Matt Cruz is without a doubt one of the most anointed and gifted Spirit-empowered leaders of his generation. This book will empower you not just to survive but to thrive as you come out of every storm with an anointing like never before. It's not just a must-read—it is a must-do.

—REV. SAMUEL RODRIGUEZ
PASTOR; AUTHOR; MOVIE PRODUCER; PRESIDENT,
NATIONAL HISPANIC CHRISTIAN LEADERSHIP CONFERENCE

Stormproof is a must-read. Matt takes his life experiences and turns them into powerful, relatable lessons that will challenge you to respond to God's Word. Matt's life is a testament to God's grace and anointing. I am so proud of you, Matt. Truly, this is my beloved son, in whom I am well pleased.

—FRANK CRUZ
SENIOR ASSISTANT PASTOR,
LIGHTHOUSE CHURCH OF ALL NATIONS

Stormproof by Matt Cruz is a challenge to develop a strong foundation of faith that withstands even life's most difficult storms. Using both biblical revelation and personal testimony, Matt writes to inspire believers to stop wading in the shallows of Christianity and dive deep into wholehearted commitment to Christ. This book will provoke you, inspire you, and leave you compelled to go all in for the Lord Jesus.

—DAVID DIGA HERNANDEZ
EVANGELIST

This book is just in time! Everything that can be shaken will be *except* those that are stormproof!

—SID ROTH
HOST, *SID ROTH'S IT'S SUPERNATURAL*

In *Stormproof,* Matt Cruz delivers a powerful and timely message about developing faith that withstands life's fiercest storms. Cruz shows us how to build an unshakable foundation in Christ, resist compromise in an age of conformity, and live with eternity in mind. This isn't just another book about faith—it's a guide to developing the kind of resilient trust in God that prevails through every season. Whether you're currently in a storm, coming out of one, or preparing for what's ahead, *Stormproof* will equip you to stand firm when the winds blow and the waves rise.

—MIKE SIGNORELLI
LEAD PASTOR, V1 CHURCH

In *Stormproof*, Matt Cruz provides an excellent road map for developing the genuine faith needed to overcome any storm. This book will comfort and challenge you, reminding you of God's presence while provoking you to go deeper. He carefully weaves together Scripture with stories in a way that ignites your faith, making your spirit stand at attention. This book inspires you to embrace the impossible and live victoriously.

—DAVID S. WINSTON
AUTHOR; PASTOR, LIVING WORD CHRISTIAN CENTER

Stormproof is a mandate for this generation—a battle cry for those who refuse to be tossed by the winds of culture, doubt, and spiritual complacency. Matt Cruz has delivered a book that is filled not just with words but with a call to action. In these pages, he lays out a powerful, Spirit-driven blueprint for anchoring your faith so that when the storms of life come, you're not just surviving—you're standing firm, unshaken, and victorious.

This isn't soft Christianity. This is fire-tested faith. Matt doesn't just write about trusting God—he's lived it. Every chapter is soaked in Scripture, personal testimony, and raw conviction that challenges you to build your life on something eternal. If you're tired of being blown around by circumstances, *Stormproof* is your guide to unshakable trust in Jesus.

I highly recommend this book for anyone who is ready to go all in, build a faith that doesn't waver, and step into the bold, immovable confidence that comes only from a life anchored in Christ.

—CHRIS GARCIA
FOUNDER, FATHER'S GLORY INTERNATIONAL;
AUTHOR, *FRESH OIL*

This generation is crying out for a Spirit-filled life teeming with power. This is a response to postmodern Christian culture, which has dampened the requirements for being a living sacrifice and eliminated power from much of the church.

In his new book, my friend Matt Cruz sounds a trumpet pointing back to a first love lifestyle that glorifies God almighty and offers the reader staying power through life's challenges. While reading *Stormproof*, it struck me that Matt has developed a high-octane devotional. Not only are there personal examples, but there's a laid-out, paint-by-numbers journey that has the potential for you, the reader, to absorb and grow from.

This book serves discipleship and a power-filled gospel. It is served by a man of God who has laid down his life to deliver principles, not from a place of theory but from a position of experience. It is refreshing to see the proof in the author's life, as Matt is a product of the gospel he offers on every page.

Many years ago the Spirit of the Lord told me that a generation of young lions would rise and lead an earthshaking reformation back to the things of God. Matt Cruz is a powerful example of this very thing. It is my honor and privilege to endorse *Stormproof*. Matt shines a fresh light on what the Lord wants to do in your life as a believer.

—JOSEPH Z
AUTHOR, BROADCASTER, PROPHETIC VOICE
JOSEPHZ.COM

STORM-PROOF

STORM-PROOF

MATT CRUZ

CHARISMA HOUSE

STORMPROOF by Matt Cruz
Published by Charisma House, an imprint of Charisma Media
1150 Greenwood Blvd., Lake Mary, Florida 32746

For more resources like this, visit MyCharismaShop.com and the author's website at mattcruzministries.com.

Cataloging-in-Publication Data is on file with the Library of Congress. International Standard Book Number: 978-1-63641-489-8
E-book ISBN: 978-1-63641-490-4

1 2025
Printed in the United States of America

Most Charisma Media products are available at special quantity discounts for bulk purchase for sales promotions, premiums, fund-raising, and educational needs. For details, call us at (407) 333-0600 or visit our website at charismamedia.com.

I dedicate this book to the precious Holy Spirit, my constant Counselor and faithful Guide. In every storm I've faced, He has been my anchor, revealing Jesus to me and shaping me more into His image. As the Master Potter, He has never given up on me, faithfully molding me through every trial and reminding me that I am a beloved child of God.

I also dedicate this book to those currently weathering storms and to all who remain steadfast in following Jesus, refusing to bow down to the idols of this world. May you stand strong in this age of compromise. God sees you, and He is with you every step of the way.

CONTENTS

PART I
BECOMING STORMPROOF

PART II
STORMPROOF STUDY GUIDE

FOREWORD

THIS IS NOT just a book—it's a heartfelt guide through life's inevitable storms. With profound insight, Matt illustrates the necessity of anchoring our faith in Christ, reminding us that even in our most turbulent seasons, we are never alone. Storms will come. The winds will rage. The waves will crash. But those who build their lives on Jesus will stand firm.

Matt's personal journey from a casual believer to a devoted follower of Jesus serves as a powerful testament to the transformative power of a deep, unwavering faith. Faith is not tested in times of comfort—it is forged in the fire, in the moments when everything around us seems uncertain. It's in these refining seasons that God strengthens us, matures us, and prepares us for what's ahead.

This book encourages us to embrace our trials as opportunities for growth rather than obstacles to our destiny. Trials are not meant to break us; they are meant to build us. They reveal the strength of our foundation and expose the areas where we must fully surrender to Christ. Matt reminds us that Jesus is the anchor that steadies our souls. When the storms rage, we have a choice—will we be shaken, or will we trust in the One who holds all things together?

What makes *Stormproof* so powerful is that Matt writes from experience. He is not just offering wisdom—he is sharing his testimony. He has walked through the storms, and he has seen God's faithfulness firsthand. His story is a reminder that when we place our faith in Jesus, no storm can destroy us. Instead, every hardship becomes a stepping stone toward greater intimacy with God and greater victory in our lives.

I highly recommend *Stormproof* to anyone seeking resilience and hope in their faith journey. If you are facing a storm, wondering how you will make it through, this book will equip you with the tools to stand strong. Let these pages remind you that with Jesus as your foundation, you are not just a survivor—you are more than a conqueror.

—VLADIMIR SAVCHUK
PASTOR, HUNGRYGEN; AUTHOR, *HOST THE HOLY GHOST*

INTRODUCTION

THIS BOOK WAS birthed during a fast at the start of 2023. During that time, I received a prophetic word from a trusted voice that I would write a book on faith. My initial response was, "That's not what I see, nor what I plan to do." Writing a book is no small task, and faith didn't seem like the topic I would focus on. But after walking through a year and a half of refining seasons, my heart began to stir with an urgency to share what I had learned.

Time and seasons have a way of molding us into who God has called us to be. Through this process I've realized that many people struggle in life's storms because they lack an anchor. They don't understand the purpose of the storms or what God is doing in them.

I believe the foundation of our faith is everything. Without a strong foundation we'll be tossed around by the winds and waves of life, unable to stand firm when hard seasons come our way. But when our faith is anchored in God, we can weather any storm and even embrace those turbulent seasons, knowing He wants to use them to reveal more of who He is, teach us valuable lessons, and ultimately shape us into His image.

This book is filled with powerful stories and fresh revelations that I pray will open your eyes to spiritual truths that can transform your life. As I've written these pages, I've gained even deeper insights from my experiences—sometimes through simple, everyday situations. God has a way of speaking through the most ordinary moments, using even the smallest details to reveal deep truths. I now see how He's been weaving everything together, and I believe He intended for me to share my experiences here to help you encounter Him in a deeper way.

As you read, I pray you'll open the door of your heart to the Holy Spirit and allow Him to take an inventory of your spiritual condition. Let Him show you what needs to be cleared out so your life can be rooted in the truth of God's Word.

To help you dig deeper, I've included reflection questions at the end of each chapter. Take time to ponder these questions and allow the truths you've read to settle in your heart. There's also a companion study guide in part 2 that you can use on your own or in a small group setting, providing an even richer experience and allowing for deeper discussions about these concepts.

This book is not just about storms. While I address them, I also dive into other key themes, including sonship, prayer, and living with eternity in mind. My hope is that you'll find language for the longings of your heart and feel a fresh stirring to pursue a deeper, more genuine relationship with God.

In the hour in which we live, counterfeit faith is everywhere. It's a faith that talks the talk but doesn't change lives. It bends to the world's standards, is quick to compromise truth, and is driven by feelings rather than the Word of God. But I believe God is awakening something in the hearts of His people, a deep stirring that brings us back to the fear of the Lord, to reverence His presence, and to live fruit-bearing lives.

As you dive into these pages, I believe you will experience that awakening. You will begin to see everything—your life, your purpose, and your relationships—through the lens of Christ. By God's grace I trust that when you reach the final chapter, your life will never be the same. You will be equipped to stand firm in life's storms, anchored in faith, and empowered to live a life that glorifies God in every season.

Let's begin this journey together. I believe that as we go deeper into the Word, we'll develop unshakable faith, stay connected to the Vine, and start living with eternity in mind.

PART I

BECOMING STORMPROOF

CHAPTER 1

THE FOUNDATION OF FAITH

I N THE GOSPEL of Matthew, Jesus tells a powerful parable:

> Therefore everyone who hears these words of mine and puts
> them into practice is like a wise man who built his house
> on the rock. The rain came down, the streams rose, and the
> winds blew and beat against that house; yet it did not fall,
> because it had its foundation on the rock. But everyone who
> hears these words of mine and does not put them into prac-
> tice is like a foolish man who built his house on sand. The
> rain came down, the streams rose, and the winds blew and
> beat against that house, and it fell with a great crash.
>
> —MATTHEW 7:24–27

This story paints a powerful picture of how important our foundation is. Jesus points out that there are two types of foundations:
one that stands strong against life's storms and one that collapses
under pressure. But what stands out to me most in this passage is
that the difference between the house on sand and the house on
rock is revealed only when the storms hit. We all build our lives
on something, and it is in times of testing that our foundation is
made clear.

Let's be honest: It can be difficult to determine if a believer is
truly living out their faith until they face a trial. Everyone appears
to be a believer when times are good. However, true faith is revealed
when we are called to trust God in life's most difficult moments.

It's during loss, disappointment, or the unexpected that we truly see the depth of a person's faith.

I'll never forget the time a few years ago when I went through a challenging period that felt like a storm. I was tossed around and struggling to find my footing. At the time, I didn't realize my foundation was weak. On the surface everything seemed great. I was experiencing God's favor, and we even held a ribbon cutting for my new studio. Friends and family flew in to celebrate this milestone, and I was filled with joy.

But once everyone left and I was alone, I felt a deep emptiness. In that moment, I got on my face and cried out to God. It was then that He revealed to me the truth: My foundation was shaky. I've learned in my walk with Christ that how we handle the hard times reveals our true character, and that difficult season exposed some cracks in mine. It was clear that I had been building certain areas of my life on sand. I was bound to rejection, and so many other issues sprung from that. The relationship I was in became an idol to me. My life was out of balance in many ways. I was putting people and things before Christ without even realizing it.

After that encounter, the Holy Spirit took me on a journey of understanding the importance of building my life on the Rock. God uses the storms of life to reveal the strength of our foundation. He does this not only to prepare us for what He has planned for us but also to shape our character to reflect His. God wants us to have true stability, and the only thing that is stable and unchanging is Jesus. He is our Rock. When our lives are built on Him, we have a foundation that can withstand even the toughest seasons.

The life built on sand, on the other hand, will inevitably fall. Sand represents things that are temporary and unreliable. Sand shifts and is unable to offer true stability. When we base our lives on things that are unstable, we build on a foundation that cannot support us in difficult seasons. Everything in this world will pass away, which means we need to focus on what lasts.

There are many people who know a lot about Christianity but

are not truly grounded in Christ. They may look and sound religious, but their foundation is weak. They're building on sand. They know the truth and can act like Christians, but they don't let God's Word change their hearts.

Become a Doer of the Word

I travel just about every weekend, and whenever I'm on a plane and the flight attendants start talking about the safety procedures before takeoff, I usually have my headphones on and am totally not paying attention. One time while I was on a flight, the Holy Spirit convicted me as I tuned out the safety instructions. Because I would so often ignore the procedures, I realized that if there was an emergency, I wouldn't know what to do.

> God uses the storms of life to reveal the strength of our foundation.

It struck me how this mirrors the way many believers treat the Word of God. We come to church week after week, hear powerful sermons, and read God's Word, but how often do we truly internalize its instructions and apply them to our lives? James 1:22 says, "But be doers of the word, and not hearers only, deceiving yourselves" (NKJV). This verse is telling us that hearing the Word without applying it is self-deception.

Just as ignoring flight safety instructions can lead to serious problems in an emergency, not applying God's Word in our lives puts us in spiritual danger. On the plane that day, the Holy Spirit pierced my heart with this truth, showing me that being a believer is not just about hearing the Scriptures; it's about actively putting them into practice.

In Matthew 7:24–27 the foolish builder is likened to those who hear the Word but do not act, and of course, when the storm comes, his house falls with a great crash. This reveals a truth we cannot ignore: It's not enough to hear God's Word; we must diligently obey it.

That's what it means to be a doer of the Word. It means applying the Scriptures in every aspect of our lives. It means loving our neighbors as ourselves (Matt. 22:39), forgiving others as we have been forgiven (Eph. 4:32), and seeking first the kingdom of God (Matt. 6:33). It means living with integrity, humility, and compassion.

We have to be careful not to become like those who hear the safety instructions on a plane but fail to apply them when needed. In Luke 6:49 Jesus says they are "like a man who built a house on the ground without a foundation. The moment the torrent struck that house, it collapsed and its destruction was complete." Again, we must be those who hear the Word and put it into practice. Jesus said, "They are like a man building a house, who dug down deep and laid the foundation on rock. When a flood came, the torrent struck that house but could not shake it, because it was well built" (Luke 6:48).

Many people avoid making an effort to build on a solid foundation. They know that building on rock requires more time, effort, and money. It's quicker and cheaper to build on sand. But the kingdom life is not cheap. There is a price to pay, and that price is your convenience.

In my first few years as an itinerant minister, I was one of these Christians. I had almost no prayer or devotional life. I was going through the motions of having a relationship with Christ but skipping important steps. I always had a pure heart, but I gained exposure and influence through social media at a young age, causing my platform to grow quickly. However, the cracks in my foundation and my lack of effort spiritually eventually were revealed when the storms came.

You see, maintaining a surface-level faith takes less time and energy than truly developing your spiritual life and producing fruit. It's simpler to attend church for an hour each week than to cultivate deep spiritual roots. It's easier to discuss sharing your faith than to actively seek opportunities to lead someone to Christ. It's easier to claim Jesus as Savior than to make Him Lord. A great friend of mine once said, "When Jesus is your Savior, you have Him. When He's Lord, He has you." A lot of people claim to be saved but deny Him by their actions (Titus 1:16). It's one thing to talk about the Word; it's another to truly live it out.

EXAMINE YOUR FOUNDATION

Take a moment to reflect on what you are building your life on. Are your choices guided by biblical values and principles, or are they driven by immediate gratification and the ways of the world? Allow God to expose your motives and reveal to you whether you're building your life on a solid foundation.

It's been said that a building will either stand or fall depending on its foundation. The same is true spiritually. As followers of Jesus we will either stand firm in the storm or fall based on the foundation we have built our lives on. We can pursue quick fixes, comfort, and shortcuts to success, or we can have true stability by staying connected to Christ and putting His Word into practice.

I meet many young people who desire to jump into ministry. I praise God that He's raising up another generation of ministers, but I also see a dangerous trend. Too many are chasing the platform without first building a solid foundation in Christ. They're hungry for recognition, for influence, for the opportunity to stand in front of people and preach, lead worship, or prophesy. But they're not getting quiet before God and letting Him shape their character.

Here's the truth: If your foundation isn't solid, everything you build on top of it will eventually crumble. We have a generation of young people who can preach, but can they live holy lives? They can prophesy, but do they honor their parents? We know how to perform ministry, but are we living in a way that reflects the heart of God? Ministry is not just about what we do in front of people—it's about who we are when no one is looking. The quality of our foundation is everything, because if it's not strong, when pressure comes, we'll collapse. I've found myself in this place many times, and looking back, I can see why I struggled for years in certain areas.

If your foundation isn't solid, everything you build on top of it will eventually crumble.

So many young people are trying to build on a foundation of sand. You can have all the gifts, all the passion, all the energy, but if your life isn't grounded in something deeper than the hype of ministry, it's all going to fall apart eventually. In 1 Timothy 4:16 Paul warns Timothy: "Watch your life and doctrine closely. Persevere in them, because if you do, you will save both yourself and your hearers."

Ministry is not just about what a person preaches—it's about how they live and why they believe what they believe. If you're a minister and you're not personally grounded in the Word of God, your ministry will not stand. We need to get to the place where we're not just practicing what we preach but also preaching what we practice.

The truth is, you won't make it far if your character is underdeveloped. The Christian life is not about the spotlight; it's about knowing Jesus and living according to the Word of God. Paul says in Colossians 2:6–7, "So then, just as you received Christ Jesus as Lord, continue to live your lives in him, rooted and built up in him, strengthened in the faith as you were taught, and overflowing with thankfulness."

I've learned through the stormy seasons that when you are rooted in Christ, you are not easily moved. But if you skip that foundational work, when storms come—whether in the form of temptation, failure, or criticism—you will find yourself shaken.

Before you reach the place where you're ministering on platforms, let God build your character. Be committed to living holy when no one's watching. If you do this, then when you stand in front of people, your ministry will be the outflow of a life already built on the truth.

Longevity in ministry comes not from your gifts and charisma but from the depth of your foundation in God. So take the time to build. This is what matters, and this is how you'll have stability and longevity in ministry and in the Christian life.

CHARACTERISTICS OF THOSE WITH A STRONG FOUNDATION

So how do you build a strong spiritual foundation? Those whose lives are anchored in the Lord demonstrate certain characteristics.

- **They seek God in prayer.** Those with a strong foundation actively engage in conversation with God. They seek His will and are strengthened by the joy of the Lord.

- **They are full of gratitude.** These believers cultivate an attitude of thankfulness, recognizing blessings and past breakthroughs, even in difficult times.

- **They lean on seasoned believers.** People with solid foundations counsel with more-seasoned saints who encourage them and share their wisdom.

- **They are rooted in the Word.** They build a reservoir of the Word within themselves so they know where to go during hard times.

- **They adapt to change.** These believers adjust to the spiritual climate they are currently in.

- **They maintain hope in adversity.** They hold on to faith and expectation, trusting God's promises during tough times.

- **They examine their hearts regularly.** They take time to evaluate their personal growth and allow the Holy Spirit to take an inventory of their spiritual condition.

We must make the effort to do what pleases God, to live a life worthy of the calling we've received. You see, even as we build our faith on this firm foundation, if we're not vigilant, we may find our hearts infested with things that weaken our faith. In the natural, if we allow ants to invade our homes, they can damage our belongings, spoil our food, and create chaos. In the same way we don't want ants taking over our homes, we must guard against the little things that can disrupt our spiritual lives.

We read about this in the Song of Solomon: "Take us the foxes, the little foxes, that spoil the vines: for our vines have tender grapes" (2:15, KJV). In Scripture the vine represents our relationship with God and the spiritual fruit we bear. Jesus said in John 15 that He is the true Vine and we are the branches, and if we remain connected to Him, we can bear much fruit.

Those who are building on the Rock must be aware of the little foxes and other nuisances that can threaten the health of their spiritual vineyard. Just as ants are tiny yet can cause massive damage in a home over time, so it is with the little foxes. Foxes are known for sneaking into vineyards and wreaking havoc, eating grapes, digging holes, trampling the vines in search of their prey. Because of their smaller size, foxes are less noticeable and can get into places larger animals can't.

In our lives these little foxes are the small sins, issues, distractions, and negative influences that can creep into our lives and spoil our spiritual fruit. They might seem insignificant, but they can be very destructive. These little foxes can be small acts of neglect, like skipping prayer time or not reading your Bible, which dim our awareness of God's presence. I've come to realize that each day is an opportunity to either depend on God or rely on myself, and the result is always either freedom or frustration.

Small grudges or unhealed wounds might seem unimportant, but they can grow into stumbling blocks in our relationships with God and others. These are the little foxes that spoil the vines.

How to Keep the Little Foxes Out

Whenever I examine my life, I now make sure to address the little foxes in order to protect my spiritual well-being. The key is staying vigilant and proactive. How do we do this? Let's consider again the analogy of ants invading a home.

Seal entry points. In the same way we would inspect our homes for cracks and openings where ants can enter, we need to examine our lives for vulnerabilities. Are there areas where negativity or temptation can creep in?

Maintain cleanliness. Keeping a clean home is essential to prevent ants from being attracted to food and waste. Spiritually, this translates to regularly cleansing our hearts and minds through prayer and repentance. Ask God to reveal any areas of clutter or sin that need addressing.

Be diligent and watchful. I once read that ants are always on the move, and they communicate with one another to find the best paths to food. We must also be vigilant to stay connected to the Vine by remaining in communication with Him.

Build a strong community. Just as ants work together, we thrive in community. We must surround ourselves with fellow believers who can support us. The Bible says iron sharpens iron (Prov. 27:17). Together, we can help one another spot the "ants" and "little foxes" that may be creeping into our lives, and we can hold each other accountable. True, godly covenant friendships are essential to our spiritual well-being.

Take immediate action. If you notice ants starting to invade, take immediate action. One time a candy wrapper somehow ended up on the rug in my room. It seemed like an army of ants came out of nowhere, trying to get to this candy wrapper. I had to get rid of it immediately to stop the ants from invading. This also works spiritually. If you identify small issues (little foxes) in your life that threaten your spiritual health, address them right away. Ask the Holy Spirit to help you recognize these vulnerabilities and make the necessary changes.

By paying attention, we can prevent small issues from growing into larger problems. We can build a life that not only stands strong on the Rock but also flourishes without interference from unwanted invaders.

A Faith Built to Last

Building your life on the Rock is not a one-time event but an ongoing commitment. It's a daily decision to trust God, apply His Word, and remain vigilant against anything that could erode your foundation.

God uses the storms of life to reveal the strength of what we have built upon. If your foundation is Christ, you will stand firm no matter what comes your way. But this requires intentionality—seeking Him in prayer, being rooted in His Word, and keeping watch for the little foxes that try to sneak in and disrupt your spiritual growth.

Jesus promised that those who build their lives on Him will not be shaken. In Him we find stability, hope, and the strength to endure. So let this be your foundation: a life anchored in Christ, producing fruit that reflects His glory and standing unshaken in the face of every trial.

Is your life stormproof?

Are you building on the Rock, or are there areas of your life where you've settled for sand? What small "foxes" have you been ignoring that could be weakening your spiritual foundation? Ask God to show you the areas that need strengthening, and commit to being a doer of the Word so you can stand firm when the storms come.

God, thank You for being the solid foundation beneath my feet. Show me the areas in my life where I've built on sand instead of rock. Reveal the small distractions or habits that may be compromising my faith, and help me address them before they grow. I want to be rooted in You not just when things are easy but especially in the storms. Strengthen my foundation, and help me live out Your Word, not just hear it. In Jesus' name, amen.

CHAPTER 2

THE ANCHOR OF YOUR FAITH

W E ALL ENCOUNTER storms in life. It's inevitable. In fact, it's often said that we're always in one of three seasons: We're either going through something, about to go through something, or just coming out of something.

That "something" is usually a stormy season in our lives. God's Word tells us that we all will experience difficult seasons. They may be seasons in the wilderness, seasons of waiting, or seasons when we wonder what God is doing. All of these experiences can shake us to our core. But when our faith is anchored in the right place, we can weather any storm.

I've learned that faith needs something to hold on to. It must have something to anchor itself to. Without an anchor, our faith will be tossed around by the winds of life. Just as a ship needs an anchor to stay secure in a storm, our faith needs to be anchored in God.

In this chapter I want to explain two ways of going through tests that the Lord showed me. In the first, we face our trials without an anchor; in the second, we endure tests with Christ as our anchor.

TEST ONE: THE TRIAL WITHOUT AN ANCHOR

Many of us have experienced times when we felt lost and shaken by life's storms. Whether we're wrestling with personal struggles, family challenges, or the weight of overwhelming responsibilities, these times can leave us feeling like ships tossed by the waves, searching for solid ground. This can feel overwhelming. I know from experience.

As a child I attended church regularly. Born and raised in a Christian home, I participated in youth groups and Sunday school all my life. I had faith. I understood that God was real and that He loved me, but I lacked a deep, personal connection to Jesus.

It was only after I radically encountered the Holy Spirit in my basement when I was nineteen years old that I realized my faith was anchored in doctrines and traditions instead of a personal relationship with Christ. It was there in that basement that I realized Jesus was not just someone to believe in but someone to fully surrender my life to.

God wants us to know Him—not just intellectually but deeply and personally. Think about it: When storms arise—problems at school, family issues, or personal struggles—what holds you steady?

Without an anchor, your faith is vulnerable to the storms of life. Remember the story of Peter walking on water? In Matthew 14:22–33 we see Peter step out on the water in faith, trusting Jesus. But when he looked away—when he let the storm distract him—he began to sink. "Lord, save me!" he cried, and Jesus immediately reached out His hand to steady him. This is a familiar story, but it is a great reminder that even when we have faith, if we're not anchored in Christ, we can start to drown in our circumstances. For a moment Peter's foundation became like sand instead of rock.

We may not realize our desperate need for an anchor when we're in this first test. This is what causes people to find peace and satisfaction in temporary things such as relationships, careers, or material possessions. Yet these are all insufficient. Each is a temporary fix that will eventually leave a person empty. This is why we must anchor our faith in God and obey His Word. Without Him as our anchor, our lives will be shaky.

Once I was in a rideshare heading home from the airport. My driver was a kind, outgoing man who asked me questions about what I do. I shared my story with him, telling him about my journey from being just a churchgoer to becoming a genuine follower of Jesus Christ. I explained that I once went through the motions of attending church but did not fully grasp what it meant to make Jesus the Lord of my life. The driver listened intently, and we soon began to talk about his own faith journey. He said he believes in God, attends church on every holiday, and prays when he passes an Orthodox church. But that's where his commitment ended.

The conversation revealed a major issue many people are facing today. They think it's enough to believe in God or attend church occasionally. But true discipleship is about surrendering everything to Jesus.

In Luke 9:23 Jesus tells us, "Whoever wants to be my disciple must deny themselves and take up their cross daily and follow me." This is not an occasional commitment where we honor God only on holidays or surrender part of our lives to Him. It's a daily, wholehearted dedication to following Jesus. It means exchanging our own plans and ambitions for His. It means being plugged into a local church, not just praying when you pass it. It means serving people well and giving generously.

In my own faith journey I discovered that being a Christian isn't just about identifying with the faith—it's about allowing Christ to be the Lord of every aspect of our lives. It means yielding to the Holy Spirit, letting Him lead us into all truth and transform us from the inside out.

During our conversation the rideshare driver said, "We are in the same boat; I'm just not hardcore about it." I left that car thinking about his words. The driver and I were indeed in the same boat in that we both acknowledged God, but there was a difference in our level of commitment.

In the Same Boat with Different Anchors

Two people can share the same boat, yet their anchors—the things that hold us firm and steady—may be very different. Some of us have anchors deeply rooted in fiery, passionate faith, while others have more loosely connected anchors that reveal a lukewarm or casual approach to God's Word.

The anchor is what grounds us in our faith. People who are deeply committed to God, actively pursuing a relationship with Him, and doers of the Word have their anchors firmly planted. It holds them steady no matter how crazy the waters are. Those with loose anchors are often tied to distractions, mixing their spiritual commitment with worldly things.

In Revelation 3:15–16, Jesus speaks to the lukewarm church, saying, "I know your deeds, that you are neither cold nor hot. I wish you were either one or the other! So, because you are lukewarm—neither hot nor cold—I am about to spit you out of my mouth." This passage points out the importance of having a firm, committed anchor rather than a half-hearted one.

> ## Being a Christian isn't just about identifying with the faith—it's about allowing Christ to be the Lord of every aspect of our lives.

Being in the same boat also doesn't mean two people are heading in the same direction. It's possible to be near Jesus in our religious practices but still distant from Him in our hearts. True faith involves more than going to church or doing good deeds. It requires a genuine connection with Jesus.

Again, it's not enough to simply be in the same boat. We must be anchored to Christ and active in our spiritual lives. We have to ask ourselves if we are truly following Jesus or just floating along. Are we God chasers, or are we content with just going through the motions?

While in Denver for a ministry conference, I remember waking up in my hotel room and hearing the phrase "left-brained generation" in my spirit. I immediately researched how the left side of the brain works and learned that *left-brained* is used to describe the way many of us think—rational, logical, and analytical. I thought about how many students today are taught to think logically and analytically. We live in a world where we want to understand everything, have answers to every question, and make sense of every situation. This is what left-brain thinking is all about. It's rational, structured, and focused on facts. It's the part of us that drives us to solve problems, control situations, and attempt to make sense of life.

But here's the issue: When we approach our relationship with God with that mindset, we often miss the more relational side of faith. We think we don't need an anchor because we are in control. We start to believe that if we just show up for church on holidays or pray when we pass by a church, we're doing enough. That's exactly what the rideshare driver thought. He said, "I believe in God, I go to church every holiday, and I say a prayer when I pass an Orthodox church."

We were both in the same boat. We both acknowledged God, but there was a difference. My faith had an anchor: a personal relationship with Jesus. His faith was loosely tied to routine actions. He thought attending church occasionally and praying when convenient were enough, but his anchor wasn't truly in Christ. It was in rituals, and those don't hold us firm when storms come.

This is where the "left-brain" mindset can mislead us. We try to make our faith fit into something we can fully understand or control. We think if we do the right things or follow the right steps, we're good. But God doesn't just want our logic—He wants our hearts. He wants to be in the driver's seat of our lives. He wants to become our anchor.

A relationship with Jesus isn't about following a religious checklist or perfectly understanding everything about God and His Word. It's about surrendering our wills to Him and letting God move in ways that don't always make sense to our rational minds. That's why we can't settle for a half-hearted faith. Like the rideshare driver, we might think we're in the same boat as others, but the reality is we're not anchored to the same thing.

When our faith is tied only to routines or a superficial devotion, it won't hold us when the winds blow hard. But when our anchor is truly in Jesus—when we go all in with Him and lay our lives down—we can weather any storm, knowing He's the One holding us steady.

The apostle Paul was once a Pharisee, trained in the most logical, structured way of thinking about God. He understood the Law and could debate theology. But while on the road to Damascus, Paul had an encounter with Jesus that transformed his life—to the point that he said, "I consider everything a loss because of the surpassing worth of knowing Christ Jesus my Lord, for whose sake I have lost all things. I consider them garbage, that I may gain Christ" (Phil. 3:8). Paul didn't meet Jesus through an argument. He had a genuine, life-changing encounter with the risen Savior that left Paul blind and stunned.

After that encounter, Paul didn't just know *about* Jesus; he knew Jesus. Paul's knowledge shifted from being logical to personal. It was no longer just about the information he knew; it was about a relationship with Jesus that changed everything.

The truth is, God doesn't call us to turn off our brains. He gave us minds to understand, reason, and think deeply. The Bible says in Romans 12:2 that God wants to renew our minds. But it also says our minds should be "transformed," not just informed.

People today need both: They need to understand the truth of the gospel *and* encounter the living Jesus. This is why Scripture tells us in Romans 10:9 "that if you confess with your mouth the Lord Jesus and believe in your heart that God has raised Him from the dead, you will be saved" (NKJV). There must be a union between our heads and our hearts.

When I was younger, my dad used to tell me that many people will miss heaven by just eighteen inches because that's the distance between their head and their heart. It's a powerful reminder that faith isn't just about understanding the truth intellectually. It's about allowing that truth to sink deep into our hearts and change how we live, love, and serve.

Encountering Jesus means stepping out of an analytical mindset where we think it's OK to be in control of our own lives and do things our own way. Instead, we need to give our hearts to the One who made them and trust in Him as our anchor. It's not just about being in the same boat but about moving in the same direction, which is us drawing near to Him.

Test Two: The Trial with an Anchor

As we grow in our faith, we come to recognize Jesus Christ as our anchor. We learn that He is our refuge and strong tower. With this understanding, we can face trials from a different perspective, knowing He will never leave us nor forsake us.

However, as believers we need to know that even with Christ as our anchor, we will go through tests. These trials may feel different. They can be more difficult, more frustrating, and sometimes more disheartening. But unlike those who face trials without Christ, we have the assurance of the presence of God. We know we are not alone.

The storms of life don't just disappear, but our perspective changes. Our understanding of God's faithfulness is what helps us endure. When I find myself in a tough season, I often have to keep reminding myself of how He has come through for me before. This helps me remember that I can rely on Him because He is faithful and unchanging.

In a world that constantly changes, it's comforting to know God remains the same. He is unchanging, and this is why we can put our complete trust in Him. The Bible tells us in Hebrews 13:8, "Jesus Christ is the same yesterday, today, and forever" (NKJV). This means His love, faithfulness, and promises are unwavering. Unlike the world around us, which can be unpredictable and unstable, God's character is steadfast.

When we face challenges or uncertainties, we can rely on His promises. God said in Malachi 3:6, "I the LORD do not change." This is very reassuring. It means God's plans for us are still good and He will never stop taking care of us. That is amazing! The God we serve doesn't shift with circumstances or moods. His commitment to you is eternal.

Think about that for a moment. God's character does not depend on how you feel! So when you feel overwhelmed, hold on to this truth: God is your Rock. You can trust Him. Embrace that He is unchanging, and find peace in knowing He will never leave you nor forsake you. Use His track record of faithfulness to stir your heart.

As Hebrews 13:8 reminds us, God's character doesn't shift or waver. His love for us is consistent. Nothing nor no one can separate you from His love. Everything around us changes—our circumstances, our relationships, even our feelings. But God doesn't change based on our performance or our situation. His love remains constant, no matter what. In other words, when God makes a promise, He keeps it. When He says He will be with us, He means it.

It's easy to question God's presence or intentions when things aren't going our way. But remember, He has promised, "Never will I leave you; never will I forsake you" (Heb. 13:5). We can trust Him, knowing His plans for us are good, even when we can't see the full picture.

In moments of doubt or fear, knowing God is our anchor gives us peace. He is steadfast and unmovable. How freeing it is to know our trust is in someone who never changes. Isaiah 26:3 says, "You will keep in perfect peace those whose minds are steadfast, because they trust in you." You find perfect peace when you trust an unchanging God and keep your gaze on Him, even in the storms of life.

Throughout the Bible there are many great examples of people who anchored their faith in God.

- *Abraham* is called the father of faith because he trusted God completely, even when what He had spoken seemed impossible. God promised him descendants, but he was old and his wife, Sarah, couldn't have kids. Yet Abraham believed, and God kept His Word (Gen. 15:6; Heb. 11:8–12).

- *Moses* didn't let fear stop him from obeying God. When God told him to lead the Israelites out of Egypt, Moses trusted God even when it seemed like there was no way out, especially when they faced the Red Sea (Exod. 14:15–31; Heb. 11:23–29).

- *David* was just a young shepherd when he stood against Goliath, a giant that everyone else was afraid of. But David knew God was stronger, so he declared, "The battle is the Lord's," and defeated Goliath with just a sling and a stone (1 Sam. 17:45–47).

- *Daniel* had such strong faith that even when King Darius made a law saying no one could pray to God, Daniel didn't back down. He kept praying and was thrown into a den of lions as a result. But God protected him, and Daniel walked out unharmed (Dan. 6:10–23).

Hebrews 11:6 says, "And without faith it is impossible to please him, for whoever would draw near to God must believe that he exists and that he rewards those who seek him" (esv).

Faith unleashes God's power in our lives!

God Uses Everything

Both ways of going through tests serve a purpose. The first exposes our need for Christ, causing us to seek Him. The second deepens our faith and causes us to grow. James 1:2–4 encourages us to consider it pure joy when we face trials because they produce perseverance.

God uses every trial to conform us to the likeness of His Son. If our faith is anchored in Jesus, tests teach us to lean on Him more fully!

Life's storms reveal how important it is that we keep our eyes on Jesus because our relationship with Him is our source of strength. The key is being captivated by His presence.

Remember, God gives perfect peace to those whose minds are stayed upon Him!

EMBRACE EVERY SEASON

I'm so grateful for the grace of God that has kept me. I've been traveling full-time for almost a decade now, and I have gone through many difficult seasons, especially in the last few years since my social media platform has grown, and those trials have really tested my faith.

I didn't understand why God allowed certain things to happen—why I had to endure so much pain and heartache. But I now realize that the purpose of the testing was to reveal what foundation I'd been building on and my desperate need for an anchor. Everyone needs an anchor, and I find it interesting that often something drastic has to happen for us to see that we can't continue in our own strength.

Today I look back and am grateful for the wounds and hard seasons because they taught me the importance of having a strong anchor in God. In the natural, when an anchor is cast into the water, it will stop the boat from drifting with the wind and current. The same is true spiritually. Christ is the anchor that steadies our souls.

He is the One who keeps us from drowning in the ways of this dying world. He is able to keep us steady when everything around us is being tossed to and fro or sinking.

Be thankful for the storms. Be thankful for the wounds because they push you toward Jesus and help build unshakable faith!

God gives perfect peace to those whose minds are stayed upon Him!

I don't know everything, but I know that when the storms of life hit—because they will—we must cling to Jesus as our anchor, knowing that God uses every season to shape our faith and character. We may not know what will happen in the next season, but we can look back on our history with God and know we can trust Him with our future.

The Lord wants to be the King of our hearts so we can produce good spiritual fruit.

Embrace the process. The best is yet to come! Remember God's promises in His Word:

> So don't try to get out of anything prematurely. Let it do its work so you become mature and well-developed, not deficient in any way.
>
> —JAMES 1:4, MSG

> All things work together for good to them that love God, to them who are the called according to his purpose.
>
> —ROMANS 8:28, KJV

As we go through different seasons, it is vital that we embrace the tests that come and let them draw us closer to God. Our trials aren't difficult for no reason. They are opportunities to grow, to better understand sonship, to know God's love for us, and to strengthen our faith.

I encourage you today: Don't let another storm pass without allowing it to strengthen your relationship with Christ. Make Him your anchor. Trust that He will be your stability in the chaos and your peace in the storm.

Is your life stormproof?

What are you putting your trust in right now? Is it something that can hold you steady, or are you drifting because you're not truly anchored in Jesus? If you've been floating along like that rideshare driver, maybe it's time to drop your anchor in Jesus.

Lord, I thank You for being my anchor in the midst of life's storms. Forgive me for the times I've looked for stability in things that cannot hold me up. I ask You to help me deepen my relationship with You. In the trials I face, remind me that You are my Rock and my refuge and that through You, I have perfect peace. Strengthen me to trust You fully, even when the winds blow and the waves rise. I surrender my heart and life to You today. In Jesus' name, amen.

CHAPTER 3

THE REFINING

RECENTLY, MY DAD and I set up a barrel sauna and a cold plunge tank in our yard. Since then, I've made sauna sessions and cold plunges a regular part of my routine. Beyond the health benefits, I've found it to be a peaceful space to think and connect with God.

One day as I sat inside the sauna, I started thinking about what happens when you stay in there for some time. The heat forces the body to sweat and bring impurities to the surface. I felt like God was showing me that fiery trials do something similar—they bring the hidden impurities in our hearts to light. Issues such as pride, bitterness, unforgiveness, and doubt rise to the surface so God can deal with them. God in His mercy allows this to happen so He can remove them, purify us, and make us more like Him.

In 1 Peter 1:7 the apostle Peter tells us that our trials are like the fire that refines gold. He says, "These have come so that the proven genuineness of your faith—of greater worth than gold, which perishes even though refined by fire—may result in praise, glory and honor when Jesus Christ is revealed."

Trials are like the heat of a sauna. They expose what's hidden.

When you sit in a sauna, the heat opens your pores, causing sweat to carry out toxins. It's the same when we go through trials. Those seasons "open the pores" of our hearts and bring up things we didn't even realize were there—fears, insecurities, doubts, or hidden sins.

This is important because God wants to remove the contaminants.

God's fire in our lives allows Him to remove what doesn't belong. These refining seasons allow us to see areas of our hearts that need to change or that need to be surrendered to Him.

What Needs to Be Washed Out of You?

One time while I was brushing my teeth and washing my face, I noticed the water rising in the sink. I went downstairs and told my dad the sink was clogged. He grabbed a wrench and some tools and headed upstairs to check it out. I sat in the bathroom, watching as he took the pipe off and discovered the gunk that had been blocking the flow of water.

In that moment, I felt God speak to me. In our walk with Him we often go through seasons when our lives feel stagnant, when the flow of joy, peace, and purpose seems blocked. These are seasons of crushing.

It's during these times that God causes us to see the hindrances that have been preventing His living water from freely flowing through us. Imagine a river whose banks are clogged with debris and rocks. Instead of flowing freely, the water becomes stagnant and murky. So it is in our lives. When we allow sin, bitterness, fear, or distractions to build up, we hinder the Holy Spirit's work within us. We have to identify the clogs. Just as a plumber identifies blockages in pipes, we have to discern what blocks the flow of God's power in our lives.

This is especially important to understand if you feel called to ministry. God desires His ministers to be vessels that are not only available and willing but also clean and emptied. A pastor once told me, "You will never be as full as you are empty." This may sound strange, but it's a profound truth. In the kingdom of God, being empty is not a sign of weakness. That's when the Lord can fill you with more of Himself. When we are empty, we create space for God's presence to pour into our lives. The more we allow ourselves to be emptied of self, pride, and distractions, the more room there is for God's presence, peace, and anointing.

Jesus said, "Blessed are the poor in spirit, for theirs is the kingdom of heaven" (Matt. 5:3). I've learned that being "poor in spirit" means recognizing our emptiness before God and acknowledging that we cannot do anything on our own and that we desperately need Him.

God cannot fill what we are not willing to empty. Think of a vessel. It's clear that a cup can hold only as much liquid as its capacity allows. If the cup is already full, there's no room for more. Spiritually, when we are full of our own desires, plans, or self-reliance, we limit what God can pour into us. But when we empty ourselves and get to the place where we can surrender our agendas to Him, He then is able to fill us with His power and love.

It's vital for us as followers of Jesus to examine areas of our lives where we might be holding on to pride or self-sufficiency. God wants to fill us with more of His Spirit, but He can't do that if we're already full of other things. When we surrender and make space for Him, we find that we are never as full as when we allow God to fill us with His presence. This is why discipleship and going through wilderness seasons are so important.

I once heard someone say, "Deliverance gets you out of Egypt; discipleship gets Egypt out of you." This struck me deeply. When you read the Book of Exodus, Egypt represents a place of bondage, slavery, and sin. It's a place where God's people were oppressed and held captive.

Moses led the Israelites out of Egypt, and they experienced freedom. For us today, deliverance is God freeing us from the grip of sin, addiction, fear, shame, or anything else that holds us captive.

But here's the truth, my friend: You can leave Egypt, but Egypt doesn't always leave you! Even after the Israelites were physically free, Egypt still had a grip on their hearts and minds. After they left, they wandered in the desert for forty long years. This was a time of crushing. They struggled with doubt, complaining, and longing for the life they left behind. Though their bodies were free, their minds and hearts were still shackled by the memories and habits of Egypt. They even dared to complain that they had all the food and drink they wanted in Egypt, as if they were better off back in slavery. It is in the refining and crushing seasons that God works in us, purging those old mindsets, those Egypt-shaped ways of thinking and living. He exposes them and begins to strip them away, all while He has us in the Refiner's fire.

God cannot fill what we are not willing to empty.

Romans 12:2 declares, "Do not conform to the pattern of this world, but be transformed by the renewing of your mind." We need to renew our minds so we stop thinking like this world, living like this world, or craving what this world craves. As the Israelites had to let go of their Egyptian mindset, we must let God remove every trace of "Egypt" in us. That's a word! Past hurts may have shaped your perspective, but we're called to think, walk, and act like Jesus. And it's in these crushing seasons—when everything feels like it's pressing in—that God opens our eyes to see through the lens of His Word!

David cried out in Psalm 51:10, "Create in me a pure heart, O God, and renew a steadfast spirit within me." That same cry must rise from our own hearts! When we make this our prayer and unclog our lives, we open ourselves for God to drive out the lingering "Egypt" in us through discipleship, surrender, and guarding our hearts. This creates space for His Spirit to flow freely within us, enabling Him to do what He desires so we can move forward in His plans for us.

When we submit to God's refining process, we come out of the fire with a pure heart and the mind of Christ. The key is understanding that the more we let God purify us, the more we reflect His glory and clear away the old mindsets and clogs in our lives.

UNDERSTANDING THE REFINER'S FIRE

I had to learn through my own fiery trials that God Himself is the Refiner. He is the One who applies the heat—not to hurt us but to purify our hearts. The impurities of sin, selfishness, and fear can't remain if we want to be effective for God. All these things have to go. Isaiah 48:10 says, "I have tested you in the furnace of affliction." God tests us through seasons of affliction to remove what is not pleasing to Him.

When you are in a period of refining, it's usually not pleasant. Just as the heat in a sauna can make you uncomfortable, trials can make you feel stretched and weak. Let's be honest: Trials push us to our limits. But they push us to confront our weaknesses, and the result is that our lives shine bright with God's glory.

It's fascinating how a person's skin glows after spending time in a sauna. As I mentioned before, the heat opens up the pores, allowing impurities to be released. After a sauna session the skin looks refreshed and has a glow. This is such a powerful metaphor for our spiritual lives. The impurities that rise to the surface during trials are not meant to stay there. God removes them because He is invested in us and wants us to shine and reflect Him.

In the Book of Malachi, the prophet speaks of the Lord as a refiner and purifier of silver.

> He will sit as a refiner and purifier of silver; he will purify the Levites and refine them like gold and silver. Then the LORD will have men who will bring offerings in righteousness.
> —MALACHI 3:3

It's incredible to me that God watches over the process so closely, making sure the silver is refined until it reflects His image perfectly. God takes meticulous care in refining our character and faith. Think about that for a moment: He is meticulous about what He began in you! He is concerned about your character and wants your life to bear good fruit.

Consider what happens to gold. When it is refined in fire, it doesn't just stay gold—it becomes pure gold, free from impurities. The same is true of us. When we are refined in the fire, our faith becomes stronger and purer.

In his first letter to the early Christians the apostle Peter compares the testing of their faith to the refining of gold through fire.

> These have come so that the proven genuineness of your faith—of greater worth than gold, which perishes even though refined by fire—may result in praise, glory and honor when Jesus Christ is revealed.
>
> —1 PETER 1:7

The trials we face—whether they are struggles in relationships, health, family, or other circumstances—are meant to remove impurities from our hearts and deepen our trust in God. Think about how rings are made. The gold or silver is heated to a very high temperature until it becomes liquid. Then, in order to remove impurities and ensure the metal is pure, it is heated again so any remaining contaminants rise to the surface, where they can be removed.

This is a great comparison to what happens in our spiritual lives during refining seasons. When we face tough trials, it's easy to question God's plan or wonder why we have to endure what we are facing. We must realize that God is using these hard times to remove contaminants and impurities. He is teaching us to depend on Him alone and molding us into vessels fit for His use!

Great things happen in times when we don't feel God moving. He's molding and shaping us. Just as impurities are removed from metal through the fire, so are we developed in fiery trials. In the Book of Romans, Paul says we are to rejoice in suffering "because we know that suffering produces perseverance; perseverance, character; and character, hope. And hope does not put us to shame, because God's love has been poured out into our hearts through the Holy Spirit, who has been given to us" (5:3–5). Trials produce endurance, character, and hope.

REFINED IN THE WILDERNESS

Something profound happens when we find ourselves in the midst of a storm, especially one that seems to come out of nowhere. I recently experienced something I'd gone more than five years without—the flu. This virus hit me like a freight train. I found myself in isolation, confined to my bedroom for an entire week, locked away so I wouldn't spread it to anyone else.

It was in that space of hiddenness, of being alone, that I felt the Lord speak something deeply to me. He often uses our natural experiences to reveal spiritual truths, and He began to show me that sickness can be like a storm, one that requires us to pause, retreat, and heal. But what was so striking to me was how much this time of isolation mirrored the seasons of wilderness and refinement God calls us into.

When we're in the wilderness, it feels like we're hidden away. There's a divine purpose in that. In much the same way I had to be locked in my room so I wouldn't infect anyone else, there are times when God brings us into a season of isolation, not to punish us but to heal us and deal with things that need to be confronted. God hides us in the wilderness because He's doing a deep work in our hearts. He's refining our character to match our calling, working on the parts of us that aren't yet fully mature and could harm others if not addressed.

If I hadn't been isolated when I was sick, I could have spread that flu, that sickness, to those around me. Similarly, if we don't allow God to refine us in the wilderness, we risk spreading the wrong things to the people around us. Our immaturity, our unresolved wounds, our unrefined character—all these things can hurt others if we don't allow God to deal with them in the secret, hidden place during these refining seasons. There's a reason God sometimes calls us away from the crowd. He's not just preserving us—He's preparing us.

Let me take this a bit deeper. When we're infected with something like the flu, our bodies go to war. Our immune system identifies the virus as an invader and starts to fight back. It not only combats the virus, but it also creates antibodies to protect us from future infection. What struck me is how similar this is to the spiritual battles we face. Every trial, every hardship, every storm we go through builds spiritual antibodies. When we face trials, we develop a resistance that helps us endure future storms. We're not just surviving—we're being strengthened for what's ahead.

I believe God wants us to understand that storms and seasons of hiddenness aren't just interruptions—they're invitations to become the people we are called to be. God doesn't waste any season. In the wilderness, He's building something in us. He's equipping us with spiritual antibodies so that when the next storm comes, we'll be able to stand firm, to remember His faithfulness, and to walk through that difficult season knowing God has a plan to bring us through.

If you're in a season of refining, a season when you feel isolated or maybe even like you're in the wilderness, know that God has not abandoned you. He is refining you. He is building something in you that will not only sustain you but also protect you in future storms. He's not just protecting you; He's preparing you. He's making you stronger to face what's ahead.

So if you're in that place right now, don't rush to get out of it. Don't try to escape. Embrace the process. Let God do His healing work. Let Him strengthen you because the wilderness is not the end; it's the place where God prepares you for the next season.

Just as antibodies in your body protect you from future viruses, every trial you face will help you grow and strengthen your faith for what's ahead. So let God do the work in you, and when it's time for you to come out, you'll be more equipped, more refined, and more prepared for what God has next.

While the Refiner's fire may be painful and make you feel like you've hit a low place, it is in these moments that God works the most in our hearts. I know that's hard to grasp, but it's true. God is working behind the scenes, though we don't sense it.

I've realized through my own experiences that hard times are not a punishment but a process of God transforming us into the likeness of His Son. He is the Master Potter; we are the clay in His hands. God cares about us so much and is so invested in us that He is committed to conforming us into His image. The Lord declared in Isaiah 48:10, "I have refined you, though not as silver; I have tested you in the furnace of affliction."

These seasons may seem dark and lonely, but God is not done with you! Dark, damp soil is exactly the environment many seeds need to grow. As the seed soaks up water in that dark place, its coat cracks open and the roots emerge. These roots anchor the plant and soak up water and nutrients that enable it to grow strong and become fruitful.

The same God who designed the seed to flourish in hidden places is the One who uses the trials of life to refine and transform us. He knows exactly what is needed to bring out the best in us. And here's something else to think about: Whether good or bad, no season lasts forever. That means the crushing season also has an expiration date! In the meantime, the Holy Spirit works through our pain, turning our trials into testimonies and our mess into messages that resonate with others. Our role is to trust Him completely, knowing that He allows us to go through tough seasons in order to refine us, strengthen our faith, and most importantly, draw us closer to Him.

MESSAGES THAT CUT

Something I believe is so important during hard seasons is hearing messages that will challenge, convict, and transform us. I call these messages that cut. They pierce our hearts deeply and cause us to renew our minds. We need to embrace these types of messages because storms are meant to lead us to genuine transformation.

The Bible tells us that the Word of God is "sharper than any two-edged sword" (Heb. 4:12, NKJV). This sword is meant to cut through our pride and sin, revealing the truth about who we are and who we are called to be. In the American church, comfort and affirmation are often prioritized. Superficial encouragement often replaces messages that drag us to the altar. Many believers today are following those who look good on the outside but have no real substance. It's not enough to look good—we must have the oil of His Spirit! That's what keeps the fire of His presence burning on the altar.

The presence and anointing of the Holy Spirit are what change people. They are the difference makers. We live in a time when charisma matters more than character, having influence matters more than having good fruit, and being liked is prioritized over being genuine. Someone can be a captivating speaker or have a large following, but that doesn't mean they carry weight in the Spirit. In 2 Timothy 3:5 Paul warns us about those who have a form of godliness but deny its power. They may appear religious, but their lives lack true connection to God.

When we follow leaders who lack substance, we risk being led astray. Their words are like ear candy, as they preach only what our flesh wants to hear. Without the anointing of the Holy Spirit, their teachings are dry and empty. I will talk more about this in chapter 6. For now, I want to stress that messages that cut us are necessary because they reveal our true condition!

If you sit back and really think about it, you'll realize that we all can be blind to our own faults and shortcomings. A message that cuts through our walls helps us see ourselves as we truly are. It confronts our preconceived notions, exposes hidden sin, and encourages us to face the flaws and offenses in our hearts. This is what leads to repentance and real, heart-level change.

Cutting messages are tough to receive. You definitely have to humble yourself and know God's intention is always to heal and restore, not to condemn. But when we allow His Word to cut through our hearts, we will find ourselves yielding to the Holy Spirit as He does a deep work in us to make us look more like Jesus.

MINISTERING IN DIFFICULT SEASONS

As a preacher, I find it can be incredibly hard to minister during tough seasons. You might find yourself wondering, "How are others experiencing blessings and joy while I feel broken?" But I know from experience that a fresh anointing comes when you minister from a place of brokenness.

In 2018 I visited Israel for the first time with my parents and home church. We toured an ancient oil press, where I witnessed the process of oil extraction. I saw a large stone being rolled over olives to crush them, and it struck me how deeply symbolic this is.

In the Garden of Gethsemane, Jesus experienced immense emotional and spiritual pain as He prayed. Scripture tells us that He sweat drops of blood, a testament to the anguish He felt in anticipation of His suffering. In this moment, He was grappling with the reality that He would soon bear the crushing weight of the sins of humanity on the cross.

The term *Gethsemane* comes from the words *gath shemanim,* which translate to "oil press."[1] This refers to a place where olives are crushed to extract their oil. This shows us that there often has to be a period of intense pain before something valuable can be released. Gethsemane is a reminder that pain and suffering lead to transformation. Jesus had to pour out in the garden so He could move forward to the cross.

It is also significant that the garden where Jesus spent His final hours before His crucifixion is located at the foot of the Mount of Olives. Just like olives, our hearts must be pressed and go through difficult times in order for us to bear fruit. There are some qualities that can only develop through hardship. I read that in ancient times olives were crushed to preserve the oil. The crushing did not destroy the olive; it protected it.

Similarly, 2 Corinthians 4:8–9 says, "We are hard pressed on every side, but not crushed; perplexed, but not in despair; persecuted, but not abandoned; struck down, but not destroyed." When we realize that the purpose of crushing is to make us into vessels fit for His use, we begin to ask God what He wants us to learn instead of wishing to avoid the pressure entirely.

If we want to be able to withstand the winds of life and win this race of faith, we must be willing to be pressed. By allowing His heart to be crushed in the garden, Jesus opened the door for us to receive salvation.

God uses trials to liberate us from things that hinder our future. Olives don't release oil until they're crushed. So too our hearts must be crushed to be fruitful. Like olives on the press, we have to go through periods of hardship to produce spiritual fruit because some things within us would never develop if we didn't go through the crushing.

Even in overwhelming moments, remember that the Holy Spirit is with you. He is your Comforter! Remind yourself of this as you continue to serve others. I've realized that the deep comfort we receive from Him during these trials enables us to be a source of comfort for others facing their own struggles. When we feel God's presence and peace during our lowest moments, we develop a deep sense of compassion for others.

God is the lifter of your head (Ps. 3:3)! When you cling to Him during these challenging seasons, your heart is stirred with empathy, enabling you to genuinely relate to another person's pain. I believe it's true when people say your story can be the key that unlocks the door to someone else's prison. Scripture tells us that the anointing destroys yokes and removes burdens (Isa. 10:27). Crushing is essential for this oil to flow! The anointing that destroys yokes and removes burdens is a byproduct of crushing seasons.

In 2 Corinthians 1:4 Paul reminds us that God comforts us so we can comfort others. Through the crushing process we become vessels of honor and living epistles read and known among all men (2 Cor. 3:2–3). I truly believe the best sermons are preached not through our words but through our lives. Those who don't know God will come to understand Him through us. We are a reflection of His glory.

God uses trials to liberate us from things that hinder our future.

When we submit to God's refining process, we come out of the fire more like Him. And the more we allow God to purify us, the more we reflect Him. So hang in there, my friend. Remember that the Refiner's fire is not meant to consume you but to transform you. Trust God's refining process because He is crafting something beautiful within you. In the end the impurities will be gone, and your life will reflect Jesus and shine with His glory!

Is your life stormproof?

In what areas of your life is God refining you through trials? What impurities or blockages is He revealing that need to be surrendered to Him? How can you embrace this process of purification to become more like Christ?

Lord, I come before You with a heart that is open to Your refining work. I acknowledge that trials are not easy, but I trust that You are using them to shape me, purify me, and make me more like You. As I walk through seasons of pressure and difficulty, give me the strength to embrace the fire, knowing that You are with me every step of the way. Remove the impurities from my heart, cleanse me from all distractions and pride, and make me a vessel of honor. I surrender my life to You, asking that Your refining fire would shape me into who You've called me to be. In Jesus' name, amen.

CHAPTER 4

THE POWER OF SONSHIP

WHILE I WAS ministering in South Texas, I had the opportunity to spend some time with the senior pastor of the church I was visiting. On my last day, before heading to the airport, we went to lunch, and he told me about his early journey with God.

For many years he believed he had to earn God's love. He tried tirelessly, but no matter how hard he worked, he never felt worthy or accepted. Eventually, he reached a breaking point. He felt exhausted from trying and, in his frustration, was ready to walk away from God altogether.

But when he was at that low place, he heard God's voice clearly speaking to him, urging him to open the Bible to Zechariah chapter 3. This was a turning point and changed everything for him. In this chapter I want to share the powerful revelation of sonship this pastor showed me through Zechariah 3, along with a few other key insights that have deeply impacted my own life.

Let's take a closer look at the passage that brought such a deep shift in the pastor's heart and consider how it applies to each of us today.

> Then he showed me Joshua the high priest standing before the Angel of the LORD, and Satan standing at his right hand to oppose him. And the LORD said to Satan, "The LORD rebuke you, Satan! The LORD who has chosen Jerusalem rebuke you! Is this not a brand plucked from the fire?"

> Now Joshua was clothed with filthy garments, and was standing before the Angel.
>
> Then He answered and spoke to those who stood before Him, saying, "Take away the filthy garments from him." And to him He said, "See, I have removed your iniquity from you, and I will clothe you with rich robes."
>
> —ZECHARIAH 3:1–4, NKJV

The vision begins with Joshua standing before God wearing filthy clothes. This represents the sin that separated him from God, just like our sin separates us from a holy God. We are all born with "dirty clothes." Romans 3:23 reminds us that "all have sinned and fall short of the glory of God" (NKJV). We all have missed the mark. And just like Joshua, we can't fix it ourselves. We can't clean ourselves up and be worthy of God's presence. Isaiah 64:6 tells us, "All of us have become like one who is unclean, and all our righteous acts are like filthy rags." God is holy, and our sin separates us from Him.

What's so amazing is that God doesn't leave Joshua in his shame. Instead, the passage says God orders that Joshua's dirty clothes be removed. He says to the angel standing nearby, "Take off his filthy clothes." Then God says, "See, I have taken away your sin, and I will put fine garments on you" (Zech. 3:4).

When we met for lunch, the pastor said with tears in his eyes, "Matt, the Lord asked me this question: Who chose to take off his dirty clothes? Was it Joshua, or was it Me?" I started to see where he was going. Just as Joshua had nothing to offer but his filthy clothes, we have nothing to offer God except our sin. But God in His mercy chooses to forgive us.

In the same way Joshua had no power to clean himself, we cannot cleanse ourselves from our sin. God chose to remove our sin and cover us with His grace. He doesn't wait for us to make ourselves right. Instead, He pursues us. And by the precious blood of Jesus,

He washes us whiter than snow, and we become the righteousness of God (2 Cor. 5:21).

Zechariah 3 continues in verse 5:

> Then I said, "Put a clean turban on his head." So they put a clean turban on his head and clothed him, while the angel of the LORD stood by.

After removing Joshua's filthy clothes, God doesn't leave him naked or exposed. He gives Joshua a beautiful new robe, which symbolizes purity and holiness. What blessed me is that by giving Joshua new clothes, God gave him a new identity, one no longer defined by sin but by God's mercy and grace.

This is a great reminder of what God does for us in Christ. Second Corinthians 5:21 says, "God made him who had no sin to be sin for us, so that in him we might become the righteousness of God." When we put our faith in Jesus, God removes our sin and gives us a new identity, just as He clothed Joshua with fine garments. This is the great exchange: He trades His perfection for our imperfection so we can be seen as righteous before the Father.

God's Choice, Not Ours

The pastor said God asked him, "Was it Joshua who decided to clean himself up, or was it Me?" It was God who chose to take off Joshua's filthy garments and give him new clothes. This shows us that we cannot earn the gift of salvation. God chooses to forgive and cleanse us. This reminds me of John 15:16, where Jesus says, "You did not choose me, but I chose you and appointed you so that you might go and bear fruit—fruit that will last—and so that whatever you ask in my name the Father will give you." He chooses us!

Our salvation isn't based on what we do but on God's grace. Ephesians 2:8–9 says, "For it is by grace you have been saved, through faith—and this is not from yourselves, it is the gift of God—not by works, so that no one can boast."

The story of Joshua in Zechariah 3 is an amazing reminder that, like Joshua, we are chosen, cleansed, and clothed by God. It's not our works or achievements that make us acceptable to God; it is only His grace. When we come before the Lord, we don't need to worry about our "filthy clothes" or our sin because God "is faithful and just to forgive us our sins and to cleanse us from all unrighteousness" (1 John 1:9, NKJV).

As God chose Joshua and made him clean, so He has chosen you and me. Hallelujah! And every day, the Holy Spirit reassures us that we are "accepted in the Beloved" and sons and daughters of the Most High God (Eph. 1:6, NKJV).

Friend, God doesn't leave us in our sin. He doesn't say, "Get yourself right before coming to Me." This is the simple message of the gospel: "God demonstrates His own love toward us, in that while we were still sinners, Christ died for us" (Rom. 5:8, NKJV). So He not only chooses us, but He saves us and gives us a new identity. God does even more than forgive our sins and make us right with Him. He adopts us into His family.

Galatians 4:4–7 says,

> But when the set time had fully come, God sent his Son, born of a woman, born under the law, to redeem those under the law, that we might receive adoption to sonship. Because you are his sons, God sent the Spirit of his Son into our hearts, the Spirit who calls out, "Abba, Father." So you are no longer a slave, but God's child; and since you are his child, God has made you also an heir.

God thought about us long before we ever thought about Him, and He chose us to become part of His family. Our new identity is being a child of God. This is the power of sonship!

Living as a son or daughter of God means many aspects of your life will change significantly. But before I go into detail about those changes, I want to share my personal journey of understanding sonship.

I began preaching at the age of nineteen, and two years later I entered full-time ministry as a traveling evangelist. For the past eight years, I've preached at numerous conferences and churches across the United States and abroad, traveling almost every weekend. However, during the first five years of my travels, I didn't fully grasp the concept of sonship, and rejection had a strong grip on my life. As I mentioned in chapter 1, God in His love showed me that my foundation was unstable. It was through understanding sonship that I finally got the clarity I needed.

Breaking the Grip of Rejection

One of the greatest battles we face is resisting the lie of rejection. When we don't fully grasp our identity as sons and daughters of the Most High God, we can easily fall into the trap of seeking validation from the world. But when we know who we are in Christ, rejection loses its power.

Rejection can be a painful experience. It leaves deep emotional scars and affects the way we live. Many issues we face in life can be traced back to the root of rejection. However, understanding our identity in Christ changes how we respond to rejection.

Knowing we are accepted and loved by God enables us to see life through a different lens. John 1:12 says, "Yet to all who did receive him, to those who believed in his name, he gave the right to become children of God."

Rejection can deeply affect how we view ourselves, but Jesus meets us where we are and offers us a new identity as His child. We see this in John 4, when Jesus meets the woman at the well. Though we never learn her name, we know she was someone who had experienced deep rejection. She had been married multiple times and was now living with a man who wasn't her husband. Others likely looked down on her, which would have affected how she viewed herself. Yet Jesus saw beyond her mistakes and shame.

This story is so powerful when it comes to understanding sonship. When the woman came to draw water, Jesus offered her something far greater—living water. He didn't condemn her but instead revealed who He was, and in seeing Him, the woman realized who she could be. Jesus didn't stop by Samaria and take a rest at the well just to quench His physical thirst. He wanted to heal the woman's emotional wounds and give her a new identity in Him.

Again, Romans 5:8 says, "But God demonstrates his own love for us in this: While we were still sinners, Christ died for us."

One of the most amazing truths is that Jesus knows who we really are. When God looks at you, He doesn't just see your failures, mistakes, or weaknesses. He sees the person He made you to be before sin came in and distorted your life. He sees your full potential in Him. This is why Jesus constantly takes the initiative to draw us back to Himself. He knows who we are meant to be.

That's why He pursues us the way He does, even when we feel broken and lost.

We may not feel good enough because of our sins or mistakes, but that's not how Jesus sees us. When Jesus looks at us, He sees beyond our failures. He sees our hearts, who we will become, and the purpose for which He designed us. This is why, despite all our flaws, Jesus never gives up on us. He is always pursuing us, even when we're running the other way.

That is one of the most beautiful things about Jesus—He's always reaching out to us. He takes the first steps. There could be one thousand steps between you and Him, and He will take 999 of those steps and leave the last one for you. He is always the One to initiate the relationship. Even when we hide from Him or feel unworthy, Jesus doesn't hesitate to pursue us with grace.

I once read an analogy that vividly illustrates what Christ does. Think of a parent who knows their child is lost. No matter how far the child runs, that parent keeps chasing after them and will stop at nothing to bring their child home. That's what Jesus does. What a powerful act of love!

The parable of the prodigal son in Luke 15:11–32 paints such a clear picture of how Jesus pursues us. The son runs away from his father, wastes everything he has, and ends up broken and desperate. Then he comes to his senses and decides to return home. What I love about this story is that when the son approaches, his father doesn't get mad and insist his son apologize for everything he did wrong before he can come home. Instead, the father runs to him, embraces him, and celebrates his son's return. This is the heart of Jesus toward us. He is always pursuing us, even when we drift or hit a low place.

WHY DOES JESUS PURSUE US?

Why does Jesus keep pursuing us, even when we fail Him or fall into sin? Because He knows who we truly are without sin. He knows who we were meant to be.

> **Despite all our flaws, Jesus never gives up on us. He is always pursuing us, even when we're running the other way.**

Jesus looks at us not based on what we've done but based on who we are in Him—a son or a daughter of God. This is why He constantly reaches out to us and is there to cleanse us, forgive us, and pick us up again. When we mess up, His heart is still to bring us back, restore us, and remind us of our true identity in Him. Knowing that God never gives up on us causes me to be filled with gratitude. He knows that beneath all the mess is the beautiful person He created. He sees beyond all the layers.

Jesus extends grace and acceptance to us, just as He did to the woman at the well, and just as the prodigal son's father (who is a picture of God) did. No matter how rejected we may feel, He offers us grace, identity, and belonging when we come to Him. We are no longer defined by our past but by who we are in Christ!

This acceptance from God is a balm for our wounds. No longer do we need to seek validation from others to feel worthy or loved. No longer do we need to please people or be bound by our mistakes. Our worth is secure in our relationship with God, and that security is like a shield against the hurt of rejection. Worry, depression, and anxiety are no longer your master—Jesus is!

I once heard a man of God say, "Your primary calling is not what you do for God; it is who you are to God." Friend, we are not defined by what we do in ministry, our failures, or the opinions of others. Our position as children of God defines us.

Knowing we are sons and daughters of God shifts our self-perception and how we live. When I finally understood my identity in Christ, my thoughts and words began to change. I stopped allowing rejection to cripple me and give me a false interpretation of people's feelings toward me. Some might ask, "How could you preach for so many years without being secure in your identity in God?" The truth is many people have a shaky foundation and don't realize it. We must recognize that sanctification is a process and discipleship is essential in our faith journey. In 1 Corinthians 1:18 Paul says, "For the message of the cross is foolishness to those who are perishing, but to us who are being saved it is the power of God." Notice that Paul says we are *being saved*. It's a present, ongoing thing. Yes, we were delivered from our sin through Jesus' sacrifice on the cross, but God is also constantly saving us, transforming us, and sanctifying us every day.

Breaking free from rejection was only the beginning for me. As I embraced my sonship in Christ, I began to see incredible changes in my identity, status, position, and relationship with God. Sonship shifts the way we live and how we interact with others. I want to point out four aspects of your life that change when you understand your sonship.

1. **Your identity.** When you choose to follow Jesus, you are adopted into God's family, and your new identity is that of a child of God. "Once you were not a people, but now you are the people of God" (1 Pet. 2:10).

2. **Your status.** At one time, you were a slave to sin with no rights (Eph. 2:1–2). Now, as a child of God, you have all the rights and privileges that come with being part of God's family. Romans 8:17 says, "Now if we are children, then we are heirs—heirs of God and co-heirs with Christ."

3. **Your position.** As a slave to sin you stood guilty before God, facing His wrath because of your sin (Eph. 2:3). But now, through Jesus, you are reconciled to God. You are holy, blameless, and free from accusation (Col. 1:18–19). You were once spiritually dead, but now you are alive with Christ (Eph. 2:5).

4. **Your relationship.** When you were a slave to sin, you lived in fear and anxiety and were blind. But as a child of God you are brought into a close, personal relationship with Him.

Isn't that beautiful? Sonship means you now gain all the rights of a child in God's family. You are His child, and nothing or no one can change that! In fact, Romans 8:38–39 tells us, "Neither death nor life, neither angels nor demons, neither the present nor the future, nor any powers, neither height nor depth, nor anything else in all creation, will be able to separate us from the love of God that is in Christ Jesus our Lord."

Now that we've seen the four key aspects of sonship, let's consider how this new identity impacts the way we live. When we truly understand that we are sons and daughters of the Most High, everything changes—including how we carry ourselves and interact with the world.

As sons and daughters of God, we are not only forgiven but also empowered to live as Christ's representatives in the earth. When you know who you are, you walk differently. And you recognize that you bring change to the environment wherever you go, infusing the atmosphere with hope.

Have you ever walked into a room that seemed quiet but then minutes later it suddenly felt full? Maybe the aisles were empty when you walked into a store, but a crowd seemed to drift in after you arrived. It's almost like the moment you show up, the atmosphere changes. People start gathering. Suddenly, things are happening that weren't happening before.

This happened to me recently while I was ministering in Dallas. I went with the pastor to lunch at a local restaurant. When we arrived, the place was completely empty. No one was sitting at any of the tables. But as soon as we received our food, I was amazed to see a long line that stretched nearly out the door. The people seemed to come out of nowhere. The crowd was so large that the manager mentioned they had never been that busy before.

This has been happening to me since I was a kid. I could be at a restaurant, a theme park, a store—you name it—and all of a sudden, a crowd seemed to form. Why does this happen? As believers we carry something in us wherever we go—the presence of almighty God. And when we show up, something in the atmosphere has to change. That is the favor of God at work in our lives.

I've learned that the favor of God isn't just about receiving blessings; it's about changing the environment around us. When God's favor rests on us, it doesn't just impact our personal lives. It impacts the atmosphere, the people we meet, and the places we go.

Psalm 5:12 says, "Surely, LORD, you bless the righteous; you surround them with your favor as with a shield." God's favor surrounds us like a shield. This means wherever we go, we are protected, and we bring favor with us. God's favor is not just for us—it's for the places we enter.

Think about it like this: When we enter a room, we bring the atmosphere of heaven. In Luke 10:5–6, when Jesus sent out the disciples, He told them, "When you enter a house, first say, 'Peace to this house.' If someone who promotes peace is there, your peace will rest on them; if not, it will return to you." Jesus was teaching that when we as believers enter any space, we bring the peace and presence of God with us! It's not just about us being in the right place at the right time; it's about what we carry on the inside.

> ## The favor of God isn't just about receiving blessings; it's about changing the environment around us.

When you understand the power of sonship, you realize that you are a carrier of hope. You are a carrier of God's presence, and that presence brings life wherever it goes. People are drawn to life. People are drawn to peace. People are drawn to hope. And the source of all those things lives inside you!

In Romans 15:13 Paul prays for the believers: "May the God of hope fill you with all joy and peace as you trust in him, so that you may overflow with hope by the power of the Holy Spirit." Hope is contagious. People who are lost, discouraged, or without purpose will be drawn to the peace and hope that radiate from your life.

I truly believe it's more about who you carry than what you say. A man of God once told me, "Matt, it's not that people are drawn to you; they are attracted to the Spirit of God inside you. It is a natural instinct for a creation to be attracted to its Creator."

When you enter a room or step on a platform to minister, people might not know what it is at first, but they will feel it. The atmosphere around you will start to change. That's the power and presence of God! Jesus is the ultimate draw, but as His representatives on earth, we too carry that drawing power.

Jesus said in Matthew 5:14–16,

> You are the light of the world. A town built on a hill cannot
> be hidden. Neither do people light a lamp and put it under
> a bowl. Instead they put it on its stand, and it gives light to
> everyone in the house. In the same way, let your light shine
> before others, that they may see your good deeds and glorify
> your Father in heaven.

You are meant to shine the light of Christ everywhere you go.
When you show up, that light fills the environment around you,
and people are drawn to that light. This is why lines form when
you walk in a room and the atmosphere seems to shift—because
you are a carrier of God's presence. You are a son or daughter of the
Most High God. Wherever you go, you bring the favor of God, the
hope of the gospel, and the peace of His kingdom.

Step into your identity as a son or daughter of God today. Find
your security in who you are in Christ. This transformation will
not only change you; it will also impact the world around you.

Is your life stormproof?

In what areas of your life have you struggled with feelings of rejection or insecurity? How does understanding your identity as a child
of God change the way you view those situations?

> *Father, thank You for the incredible gift of sonship. I
> thank You that because of Jesus, I am no longer defined
> by my past mistakes or the rejection I've faced, but by
> who I am in You. Help me to walk in the fullness of my
> new identity, fully secure in Your love and grace. I ask
> that Your peace, favor, and presence would surround
> me wherever I go, bringing change to the environments
> I enter. Help me see myself the way You see me—fully
> accepted, loved, and chosen. In Jesus' name, amen.*

CHAPTER 5

UNCOMPROMISING FAITH

I F THERE'S ONE story in Scripture that truly exemplifies uncompromising faith, it's the account of Shadrach, Meshach, and Abednego in Daniel 3. One of the first sermons I ever preached was based on this powerful passage. You've likely heard their story, but let's dive deeper to uncover key lessons about standing firm in faith.

These three young Hebrew men didn't just face a literal fire—they were caught in the middle of a spiritual battle. And boy, was their faith tested.

King Nebuchadnezzar of Babylon had conquered many nations, including Israel, and taken many people captive. As part of his strategy to control them, he attempted to brainwash them and reshape their identity by changing their names.

In biblical times, names carried deep significance. They weren't just labels; they reflected a person's identity, character, and calling. By changing the names of the Hebrew captives, Nebuchadnezzar sought to strip them of their identity in God and redefine them according to Babylonian culture and pagan gods.

This is what happened to Shadrach, Meshach, and Abednego.

- Hananiah ("God is gracious") became Shadrach ("command of Aku," a Babylonian moon god).[1]

- Mishael ("Who is what God is?" or "Who is like God?") became Meshach ("Who is as Aku is?" or "Who is like the moon god?").[2]

- Azariah ("Jehovah has helped") became Abednego ("servant of the god Nebo").[3]

The Babylonians hoped these new names would pressure the young men into abandoning their faith. But while Babylon tried to rename and reshape them, their true identity in God remained unshaken.

I'm so grateful that God does not define us by our circumstances or by the labels others place on us. He calls each of us by our true name and identity in Him.

The enemy still works the same way today, attempting to label us by our sins, failures, or weaknesses. But remember this: *The devil is a liar.* God sees past every false label and every lie of the enemy, seeing instead the identity He created for you and the person He called you to be.

THE FIERY FURNACE: A TEST OF UNCOMPROMISING FAITH

The test of the young Hebrew men's faith came when King Nebuchadnezzar set up a massive golden statue and commanded everyone to bow down in worship. Shadrach, Meshach, and Abednego were the only ones who refused. They knew the consequences—disobedience meant being thrown into a fiery furnace—but they stood firm.

When King Nebuchadnezzar confronted them, their response was amazing:

> If we are thrown into the blazing furnace, the God whom we serve is able to save us. He will rescue us from your power, Your Majesty. But even if he doesn't, we want to make it clear to you, Your Majesty, that we will never serve your gods or worship the gold statue you have set up.
>
> —DANIEL 3:17–18, NLT

These three men had uncompromising faith. They were willing to follow God even if it cost them everything. They trusted Him even when they didn't know the outcome.

That's faith! It's trusting God no matter what happens. Sometimes He delivers us by taking us through the fire, not away from it. And like Shadrach, Meshach, and Abednego, we must stand firm and declare, "Even if He doesn't rescue me, I will not bow!" Daniel 3 continues,

> Then Nebuchadnezzar was furious with Shadrach, Meshach and Abednego, and his attitude toward them changed. He ordered the furnace heated seven times hotter than usual and commanded some of the strongest soldiers in his army to tie up Shadrach, Meshach and Abednego and throw them into the blazing furnace. So these men, wearing their robes, trousers, turbans and other clothes, were bound and thrown into the blazing furnace. The king's command was so urgent and the furnace so hot that the flames of the fire killed the soldiers who took up Shadrach, Meshach and Abednego, and these three men, firmly tied, fell into the blazing furnace.
>
> —DANIEL 3:19–23

The Bible tells us the fire was heated seven times hotter than usual; it was so intense that the soldiers who threw Shadrach, Meshach, and Abednego into the furnace were killed by the heat. Isn't that something? The very trap set for these Hebrew men became the snare that destroyed their enemies!

But something amazing happened inside that furnace: God was with them. He literally showed up in the fire.

As I've mentioned before, God doesn't always deliver us from the fire. Most of the time, He walks through it with us. The fire didn't harm the men. In fact, it burned off their chains and set them free.

You may be going through a fire right now. It could be sickness, financial problems, a broken relationship, or spiritual warfare. But know this: As I mentioned in chapter 3 when I talked about the heat of the sauna, God uses fire to purify us. The heat isn't meant to destroy you; it leads to your liberation. He uses fire to free you!

One thing I've learned is that when I go through the fire, the fire of God inside me burns brighter than the fire around me. In the fire, anything that doesn't belong to God gets burned away. Sometimes we pray for God to save us from the fire, but His plan is to use the fire to transform us and bring us through it stronger than before.

THE POWER OF PRAISE IN THE FIRE

In Daniel 3:21 we see that Shadrach, Meshach, and Abednego were bound before they were thrown into the furnace. Why is that significant? Because the enemy always seeks to keep you from using your greatest weapon—your praise. If he can tie up your hands, he can try to stop you from worshipping God. But here's the truth: Even in the fire, praise is your weapon, and worship is the password to your breakthrough.

One of my evangelist friends often says, "Praise is your down payment for breakthrough!" Worship is a weapon the enemy cannot stand against. He will do everything he can to bind your hands, silence your voice, and keep you from praising God. But here's the good news: The fire you're facing can't stop your worship—it can only make it stronger.

Even though the enemy tried to bind them, Shadrach, Meshach, and Abednego could still praise. And in that moment, as they stood in the furnace, Jesus showed up. The king looked into the fire and saw them walking freely with a fourth man, and he was amazed! God often uses the fire to reveal His presence in a way nothing else can.

I want to challenge you today to stand firm in your faith, even when the world pressures you to compromise. We live in an age where people are bending the truth, trying to change God's Word, and trading their values to fit in.

We live in a world where evil is celebrated and good is condemned.

But as followers of Christ, we are called to be set apart. Just like Shadrach, Meshach, and Abednego, we must be fully persuaded of God's promises, no matter what the world says or does.

THE AGE OF COMPROMISE

Compromise is dangerous. It weakens your witness and robs you of the power of the Holy Spirit in your life. Consider Adam and Eve, Esau, Samson, David, and many others in the Bible. Compromise led to their downfall. Every time they compromised, they lost something precious.

> **Even in the fire, praise is your weapon, and worship is the password to your breakthrough.**

Today, compromise is everywhere. People twist Scripture to fit their own ideologies, leading others astray. The church is growing more lukewarm, and many believers are just going along with it. But I want to remind you that a compromised faith is a weak faith.

Looking at the lives of Shadrach, Meshach, and Abednego and the fiery furnace they faced, we see a picture of the type of faith we desperately need today—faith that doesn't bend or bow; faith that stands firm on God's promises, no matter the cost.

Christianity isn't about staying positive; it's about being Christlike. It's about taking up your cross and following Jesus regardless of the cost.

God is calling us to have uncompromising faith. What does this look like? An uncompromising Christian:

- doesn't conform to the world's standards—their goal is to be like Jesus.

- loves God with all their heart, soul, mind, and strength.

- separates themself from ungodliness.

- walks in holiness, guided by God's Word.

- says no to sin and yes to righteousness.

So let me ask you: Are you compromising? Are there areas of your life where you've bowed to the pressure of this world? If so, now is the time to rise up and take a stand. God honors those who stand firm. Just as He promoted Shadrach, Meshach, and Abednego after the fire, He will honor you when you stand steadfast in your faith.

DON'T BOW TO SIN—KILL YOUR LION AND BEAR

One day, I was running late, hoping to make it to the airport just in time for my flight. I planned to arrive a few minutes before boarding, so I thought, "I can still make it—no big deal." But when I got there, the line at security was long, and I quickly realized I was cutting it way too close. In fact, I almost missed my flight.

As frustrating as that was, it got me thinking about how we sometimes approach sin in our lives. We often want to see how close we can get to temptation without actually falling into it. We try to dance around the line of sin. But just like my airport situation, the closer we get to the line, the more we risk everything.

We are told to flee from sin, not to get as close as possible to it. Paul also warns, "Flee the evil desires of youth" (2 Tim. 2:22).

When we try to walk that fine line, it's dangerous, and it affects our fellowship with the Lord. Romans 6:23 says, "For the wages of sin is death, but the gift of God is eternal life in Christ Jesus our Lord" (NKJV). Sin always comes with a cost, even if we think we can dodge it.

Don't risk everything by getting too close to sin. We need to follow Paul's advice: "Run from all these evil things" (1 Tim. 6:11, NLT).

The best way to avoid sin is simply not answering when temptation calls. Refuse to bow. It's in those private moments when no one is watching that your battles over sin and temptation are either won or lost.

I've made plenty of mistakes over the years, and through trial and error I've learned a lot of valuable lessons. I want to share a few of them with you.

1. Kill your lion and bear in private.

In 1 Samuel 17, when David was still a young shepherd, he faced two wild animals—a lion and a bear—while out in the fields with his sheep. These weren't public battles. No one was watching him. But David knew God was watching. He had to defeat his lion and bear in private before he could face Goliath in public.

Don't risk everything by getting too close to sin.

David said to Saul in 1 Samuel 17:36, "Your servant has killed both lion and bear; and this uncircumcised Philistine will be like one of them, seeing he has defied the armies of the living God" (NKJV). David had already built a history of fighting in secret, and when the time came for a public battle, he was ready.

This is a lesson for us all. The battles you fight when no one else is around—those small victories over sin, pride, or temptation—prepare you for what's to come. God sees what happens in the secret places, and He rewards openly those who seek to please Him when no one is watching.

2. Refuse to bow even when temptation is strong.

Shadrach, Meshach, and Abednego knew the pressure of standing firm in the face of temptation. In a time when everyone else bowed to the golden image of King Nebuchadnezzar, these three men refused. When the music played and the command was given to bow, they stood firm.

When temptation comes, you have to choose not to bow. It may seem like everyone else is bowing down to sin, compromise, or things that feel easier, more comfortable, or more acceptable. But you can't bow. Just like the three Hebrew boys, your refusal to bow will set you apart.

3. God sees your private battles and will elevate you.

In those moments of temptation, remember that God sees the battle, even if no one else does. I've learned that choosing righteousness in secret is what prepares you for the public rewards. God is watching how you respond when no one else is around.

Once, God spoke to me and said, "Show Me you love Me by how you live in secret and how you treat those around you." I'm grateful for the grace and mercy of Jesus that picks us up when we fall. There have been many times in my life when I've missed the mark, but through my stormy seasons I learned how to kill my lion and bear.

God elevates those who are faithful. When you kill your lion and bear, when you choose not to bow to temptation in private, God will elevate you. Your faithfulness to say no in private prepares you for promotion in public.

Shadrach, Meshach, and Abednego were thrown into the fiery furnace, but they weren't burned. In fact, the king himself saw the fourth man in the fire and said, "Praise be to the God of Shadrach, Meshach and Abednego!" (Dan. 3:28). It's amazing how their refusal to bow led to a public demonstration of God's power.

Just as David was elevated after defeating his lion and bear, and just as Shadrach, Meshach, and Abednego were elevated after they survived the fiery furnace, you too will be elevated when you refuse to bow to sin and choose to stand firm on God's Word. God sees the small, private victories, and He will use them to promote you when the time is right.

Friend, if you want God to move in your life and bring promotion, let the fire refine you. The fire is not meant to destroy you but to purify you. When you pass through it, you'll emerge stronger, purer, and more like Jesus.

And though it won't be comfortable, you won't be alone. Isaiah 43:2 reminds us of God's promise: "When you pass through the waters, I will be with you; and when you pass through the rivers, they will not sweep over you. When you walk through the fire, you will not be burned; the flames will not set you ablaze."

Let's rise up in uncompromising faith. Let's be a generation that refuses to bow to the pressures of this world and instead stands firm on the promises of God. The fire is not the end—it's the beginning of your promotion!

Is your life stormproof?

Reflect for a moment and ask yourself, Where have I compromised in my faith? Are there areas in your life where the pressures of this world have caused your focus to shift from God? What steps could you take to stand firm in your faith, unwavering and bold no matter the cost, as Shadrach, Meshach, and Abednego did?

> *Father, thank You for the powerful example of Shadrach, Meshach, and Abednego. Their courage in the face of the fire reminds me that my faith is not meant to bend or bow to the pressures of this world. Lord, I ask that You help me stand firm in my beliefs, unshaken by fear or compromise. Empower me to trust You fully, even when the fire is raging around me. Teach me to live a life that boldly reflects Your truth and love, no matter the cost. I surrender my heart to You today, and I choose to live for Your glory above all else. In Jesus' name, amen.*

Chapter 6

COUNTERFEIT FAITH

ET's FACE IT: The Western church—especially in America—has gained a reputation for being lukewarm. We've all heard the phrase "lukewarm Christianity," but what does that really mean? Why does it seem that so many believers today have grown complacent, lacking a vibrant prayer life, discernment, and a faith they truly live out each day?

Jesus says in Matthew 7:21–23, "Not everyone who says to me, 'Lord, Lord,' will enter the kingdom of heaven, but only the one who does the will of my Father who is in heaven. Many will say to me on that day, 'Lord, Lord, did we not prophesy in your name and in your name drive out demons and in your name perform many miracles?' Then I will tell them plainly, 'I never knew you. Away from me, you evildoers!'"

These words remind us that it is not enough to just go to church or talk about God on our social media pages. You can attend every service, volunteer in every ministry, and still find your life bearing no real fruit. When Jesus says, "I never knew you," He's shaking us awake to the fact that our relationship with Him is what matters most. Too many believers get caught up in everything else yet never take the time to know Christ for themselves.

The story of the rich young ruler in Matthew 19 is a clear picture of this (vv. 16–22). He claimed to have kept all the commandments and asked Jesus what he still lacked. Jesus told him, "If you want to be perfect, go, sell your possessions and give to the poor, and you will have treasure in heaven. Then come, follow me" (v. 21).

When he heard that, the young man walked away grieving because his heart was ruled by his possessions. Jesus' challenge revealed his true loyalty.

Today there exists a gospel in America that serves us instead of changes us. It promises benefits without transformation and comfort without conviction. This version of Christianity has become comfortable with the status quo. It tells us we can have all the blessings of God without embracing the call to change.

It's disheartening that so many sermons today are tailored to meet our needs, desires, and preferences. This gospel promises joy without struggle, success without surrender, and blessings without the need for sacrifice. It's a counterfeit gospel that emphasizes self-help and immediate gratification. In America, cultural Christianity has become all too common. We are proud to say we are Christians on social media, but there is no self-denial in our daily lives.

Why do so many preachers focus on the blessings and benefits of salvation while neglecting the call to repentance, holiness, and discipleship? A. W. Tozer once wrote, "In many churches Christianity has been watered down until the solution is so weak that if it were poison it would not hurt anyone, and if it were medicine it would not cure anyone!"[1] This feel-good gospel suggests that following Jesus is about personal gain rather than surrendering to His lordship. It's more focused on what God can do for us than on how He desires to transform us from the inside out.

To determine whether you're truly subscribing to this gospel, look at the fruit in your life. The evidence of a surrendered life is the fruit you bear. The most powerful sermons we can preach are not spoken with our words but demonstrated through the way we live. Romans 8:29 says, "For those God foreknew he also predestined to be conformed to the image of his Son, that he might be the firstborn among many brothers and sisters." Those who truly reflect Jesus will always bear good fruit in their lives.

ATTENDANCE WITHOUT TRANSFORMATION

Many Christians think simply attending church or participating in conferences makes a significant difference in our lives. While these practices are important, they are not the ultimate target of the enemy. What truly alarms the devil is when we begin to reflect the character and nature of Christ. The enemy isn't threatened by a crowd of people going through the motions; he's terrified of the church becoming like Jesus! He knows that attending church or conferences alone does not necessarily lead to transformation.

It's good to have church services and conferences as part of our routine, but if that's where we stop, we'll never tap into the life-changing power that comes from fully surrendering our hearts to God. The devil isn't worried about a packed church or a well-attended conference. What truly terrifies him is when we walk out of those meetings and genuinely embody the character of Christ!

And it's not just passive churchgoers who are missing the mark; there are far too many "hirelings" in the church. A hireling is someone who shows up for a paycheck or recognition, fulfilling tasks without any real connection to the heart of God. They may be active and serve tirelessly, but their relationship with God is distant. There is no real fruit in their lives because they are not rooted in Him.

The problem with hirelings is that they may look busy, even faithful, but their work is done out of obligation, not out of love for God. When we become too comfortable, we are tempted to live a version of Christianity that asks nothing of us. We want a gospel that makes us feel good, that doesn't disrupt our lives too much. But the gospel is not about comfort; it's about transformation. Jesus did not die to make us comfortable; He died to make us holy!

We can no longer be satisfied with messages that appeal to our desires rather than challenging them. So many in the American church today need a reality check: We don't change God's Word; His Word changes us! That's why God is separating the saints from the ain'ts, the clean from the unclean, and the holy from the unholy.

Too many are focused on what people can do—how gifted or talented they are, how well they speak, or how they captivate the room. But in God's eyes, there's something more important than the gifts people carry, and that's the fruit they bear.

> # What truly alarms the devil is when we begin to reflect the character and nature of Christ.

Matthew 7:20 tells us, "By their fruit you will recognize them." Yet many of us focus more on our gifts than on the fruit that should flow from knowing the Lord.

Let's look again at Jesus' words in Matthew 7:21–23:

> Not everyone who says to me, "Lord, Lord," will enter the kingdom of heaven, but only the one who does the will of my Father who is in heaven. Many will say to me on that day, "Lord, Lord, did we not prophesy in your name and in your name drive out demons and in your name perform many miracles?" Then I will tell them plainly, "I never knew you. Away from me, you evildoers!"

These people had gifts. They were prophesying, casting out demons, and working miracles. But Jesus said He didn't know them. Why? Because although they were operating in their gifts, they weren't producing the fruit of the Spirit, the true evidence that someone is walking with God.

Gifts can be impressive, but it's the fruit that reveals where we are spiritually. The fruit of the Spirit is the outward evidence of our connection to God. In John 15:4–5 Jesus emphasizes the importance of staying connected to Him:

> Remain in me, as I also remain in you. No branch can bear fruit by itself; it must remain in the vine. Neither can you

bear fruit unless you remain in me. I am the vine; you are the branches. If you remain in me and I in you, you will bear much fruit; apart from me you can do nothing.

In other words, if we are truly walking with God, we will naturally produce the fruit of His Spirit: "love, joy, peace, forbearance, kindness, goodness, faithfulness, gentleness and self-control" (Gal. 5:22–23). These are the true indicators of whether we're spending time with God. They are the evidence that we're becoming more like Jesus.

Think of it this way: You might be amazed at how powerfully someone preaches or how they flow in the gifts of the Spirit. But the fruit is what tells you if that person's life is truly pleasing to God. Gifts may impress people, but fruit is what matters to the Lord because it reflects who He is.

Gifts Work Even When You Don't

Gifts can work even when we don't. They are given by God. Romans 11:29 says the gifts and calling of God are irrevocable. A person can have a powerful gift to preach or teach, but that doesn't mean they're connected to the Vine.

Bearing the fruit of the Spirit requires us to stay connected to the Vine. It requires us to show up in the secret place and fellowship with the Lord. People don't automatically bear fruit because they have a spiritual gift. They bear fruit because their lives are yielded to God.

Jesus said in Luke 6:43–45,

No good tree bears bad fruit, nor does a bad tree bear good fruit. Each tree is recognized by its own fruit. People do not pick figs from thornbushes, or grapes from briers. A good man brings good things out of the good stored up in his heart, and an evil man brings evil things out of the evil stored up in his heart. For the mouth speaks what the heart is full of.

It's not enough to be gifted. We must examine the fruit we're producing. If you're not producing the fruit of the Spirit, ask yourself, Am I truly connected to the Vine? It's an important question because your fruit will reveal how deeply you're connected to Christ.

The church often celebrates gifts, talents, and charisma, but what will truly matter at the end of your life is the fruit you've borne. We have to start focusing less on the gifts we carry and more on the fruit we bear. The enemy is fine with us pretending to be spiritual as long as it doesn't lead to real, heart-level change.

In 2 Timothy 3:5 Paul warns of those who have a form of godliness and deny its power. He goes so far as to say, "Have nothing to do with such people." Having a form of godliness means going through the religious motions without allowing the gospel to penetrate one's heart. It's about following routines that may look good on the outside but lack the power to change us inside.

COUNTERFEIT FAITH VS. GENUINE FAITH

In Acts 8 we see two men respond to the message Philip preached: Simon the sorcerer and the Ethiopian eunuch. These two men illustrate the difference between counterfeit and genuine faith. Simon's faith was superficial, focused on appearances and personal gain, while the eunuch's faith reflected true transformation of the heart.

Let's look first at Simon.

> When Simon saw that the Spirit was given at the laying on of the apostles' hands, he offered them money and said, "Give me also this ability so that everyone on whom I lay my hands may receive the Holy Spirit."
>
> Peter answered: "May your money perish with you, because you thought you could buy the gift of God with money! You have no part or share in this ministry, because your heart is not right before God."
>
> —ACTS 8:18–21

Simon was captivated by the signs and wonders Philip performed and wanted to be part of what Philip was doing. But Simon didn't really care about surrendering to God; he wanted the power and recognition that came with miraculous works. Simon's motives were impure and exposed his counterfeit faith—he was more interested in the benefits of the gospel than a relationship with Jesus.

> **The church often celebrates gifts, talents, and charisma, but what will truly matter at the end of your life is the fruit you've borne.**

True faith is not about how you appear to people or how much you think you know about God. It's about allowing your heart to be transformed. That's the difference between counterfeit and real faith. Real faith changes your heart. James 2:19 says, "You believe that there is one God. Good! Even the demons believe that—and shudder." Satan himself knows Scripture. He knows God is real and understands who Jesus is, but he will never trust in or surrender to God.

Many people mistakenly believe that being busy doing religious activities makes them right with God. But if those actions don't lead to heart transformation, they are meaningless. In Matthew 23:27 Jesus called out the Pharisees for this very thing, saying, "Woe to you, scribes and Pharisees, hypocrites! You are like whitewashed tombs, which indeed appear beautiful outwardly, but inside are full of dead men's bones and of all uncleanness" (MEV). He's saying in essence, "You look good on the outside, but inside you're full of hypocrisy."

Is Jesus describing you when He says this? Are you like a whitewashed tomb—doing religious works to look good on the outside while your heart remains unchanged? Genuine faith isn't about impressing others or trying to earn God's favor. It's about surrendering fully to Him, realizing you are nothing without God and desperately in need of His grace.

Without this kind of heart-level change, your faith is hollow. It doesn't matter how many Bible verses you've memorized, how often you attend church, or how many good deeds you perform. If your heart hasn't been TRULY transformed by the gospel, you're no different from Simon—using faith for personal gain rather than embracing the life-changing power of God.

The Ethiopian eunuch was so different from Simon (Acts 8:26–40). When he heard the gospel, it didn't just stay in his head; it pierced his heart. He didn't hesitate to respond to God's call. In fact, when he and Philip passed some water, the eunuch gave an order to stop the chariot and said, "Look, here is water. What can stand in the way of my being baptized?" (v. 36). His faith was real. He trusted God with everything he had and experienced heart-level change.

Don't settle for a counterfeit faith. Don't just go through the motions. Ask God to change your heart. Surrender your life completely to Him, and let the gospel move from your head to your heart.

Romans 12:2 says, "Do not conform to the pattern of this world, but be transformed by the renewing of your mind. Then you will be able to test and approve what God's will is—his good, pleasing and perfect will." This is what troubles the devil—when believers die to self, crucify their old nature (Gal. 2:20), and become more like Jesus.

THE SUNBURN OF THE SOUL

In 2023 I was on a beach in San Diego playing sand volleyball with some friends. I was having a great time, but there was one problem: I forgot to apply sunscreen.

As the day went on, the sun's rays beat down, and I ended up with a painful first-degree sunburn. The discomfort was intense, unlike anything I had ever experienced. After some research I discovered that I was battling what is known as "hell's itch," a rare condition caused by severe sunburns. Eventually I went to urgent care, where the doctor confirmed my self-diagnosis and recommended something to soothe my skin.

In the midst of this painful ordeal, God revealed a powerful truth to me. He said, "The longer you were exposed to the sun, the more uncomfortable you became with your flesh." The pain reached a point where I could no longer ignore it—I had to do something about what I was feeling, which is how I ended up at urgent care.

Here's what God showed me: Just as I became increasingly uncomfortable with my flesh under the sun's exposure, so too do we become uncomfortable with our old ways when we are exposed to the light of God's presence. The light of the Son, Jesus Christ, reveals the flaws and sins we might ignore. When we stay in God's presence, our old patterns of thinking and living start to feel unbearable.

The sunburn experience didn't stop there. Afterward, my skin began to peel and shed. This led to another profound lesson: As we dwell in the light of God's presence, we begin to shed our old selves, much like the skin peels away from a sunburn. The process might be uncomfortable, but it is necessary for healing.

The light of Christ exposes our imperfections but also invites us to grow. In the same way I had to go to urgent care to relieve my sunburn, we are called to take action in response to the discomfort we feel in the light of God's presence. That action is called repentance—to shed our old ways and embrace a new life in Him.

Unfortunately, in America we have a hard time giving up things that are convenient. I believe people resist change because they focus on what they'll lose instead of what they have to gain. When you say yes to Jesus and allow Him to transform your heart, you will lose some things. People will misunderstand you, relationships will change, and you might lose support. You will even face hatred from the world.

But here's the truth: You also gain when you choose to follow Jesus. You'll receive His provision, favor, protection, peace, validation, and so much more. In fact, what you gain in Him will far outweigh anything you lose on this earth! It's time to fully surrender to Jesus. It's amazing to me that people around the world are dying for Jesus while Christians in America are struggling to live for Him.

> **If I seek God for what He can give me rather than for who He is, my relationship with Him becomes transactional rather than transformational.**

In many parts of the world believers face persecution, danger, and even death because of their faith (see Appendix D). Their commitment to Jesus is so deep that they are willing to sacrifice everything for Him. They understand that what they'll gain in Him is better than anything they could lose in this world—even their lives!

In America the challenge is not persecution but complacency. We are blessed with freedom and comfort, yet we find ourselves struggling to fully give God our lives and be devoted to Him. Our challenge in America is to be doers of the Word in the midst of distractions and perversion.

The hour we are living in demands more than a casual faith. Our faith cannot be a part of our lives; it must be our main priority. If our relationship with Jesus is not alive and active, we will find it difficult to push through the storms and temptations that come our way.

Friend, a shallow faith will not sustain us in the midst of hardship or in moments of spiritual warfare. This is why we need the cross to be preached from the pulpit! In this hour there's a growing need for us to return to the core message of Christianity, which is that Jesus Christ died on the cross, conquered sin, and made it possible for mankind to spend eternity with Him. It is by preaching the cross that we pull people from the pit and point them to Jesus.

True discipleship requires self-denial and a willingness to embrace the cross, not just the blessings. The self-serve gospel popular in many congregations overlooks this call to sacrifice, focusing instead on how Jesus can make our lives better right now.

I had to realize that if I seek God for what He can give me rather than for who He is, my relationship with Him becomes transactional rather than transformational. A gospel that serves us rather than changes us fails to produce the fruit of the Spirit. It avoids the hard teachings of Jesus, which leads to a comfortable but powerless Christianity. I believe encouraging messages are vital, and I truly value them. But what I really need is a message that will drag me to the altar, where I can encounter the transforming power of God in my life.

The cross of Jesus is the foundation of the Christian faith. As Paul says in 1 Corinthians 1:18, "For the message of the cross is foolishness to those who are perishing, but to us who are being saved it is the power of God."

The message of the cross offers hope and redemption. In understanding Jesus' sacrifice, we find true liberation from sin and the power to change. Paul says in Galatians 2:20, "I have been crucified with Christ and I no longer live, but Christ lives in me." This means that through the cross, our old selves die and we are reborn to a new life in Christ.

We cannot embrace the cross and hang on to old ways. Our changed lives speak of the power of the cross!

In a world where people often seek only the parts of the Bible that comfort them, it's vital that we as believers embrace the full counsel of God's Word—not just His promises but also the convicting parts, the warnings, the instructions for righteous living, and the call to holiness.

Speaking to the elders of the church at Ephesus, the apostle Paul says in Acts 20:27, "For I did not shrink from declaring to you the whole counsel of God" (ESV). Paul was reminding them that he did not pick and choose which parts of God's message to share.

The *whole counsel* addresses every area of life. It speaks about our relationship with God, our relationships with others, how we carry ourselves, our work, our families, and our worship.

Second Timothy 3:16–17 says, "All Scripture is breathed out by God and profitable for teaching, for reproof, for correction, and for training in righteousness, that the man of God may be complete, equipped for every good work" (ESV). God's Word is relevant and necessary for every area of life. We need all of it—both the parts that comfort and the parts that challenge us.

Many follow this gospel of convenience because they don't know God's Word. They read it only occasionally, more out of obligation than adoration. We need to take a page from the psalmist, who said, "Oh, how I love your law! I meditate on it all day long" (Ps. 119:97).

We need a fresh desire for the Word of God to burn in our hearts. We shouldn't read it out of obligation but because we want to. When you stop viewing the Bible as a rule book and start seeing it as a way to know God, your desire to read the Word will grow.

Again, Psalm 119:97 says, "Oh, how I love your law!" Notice the psalmist isn't saying, "I read Your law because I have to." He's saying, "I love it." Love changes everything. The Bible is a treasure of truth that is alive and active. As you read it, it begins to read you, speaking directly to your current season. Every page is an invitation to draw closer to God, understand His ways, and discover His plan for our lives.

When we approach the Bible with adoration, we begin to see it not simply as a book but as something that is living and active and sharper than any two-edged sword (Heb. 4:12), that speaks to our hearts, convicts us to our core, and causes us to change our ways. God says in Jeremiah 23:29, "Is not my word like fire, declares the LORD, and like a hammer that breaks the rock in pieces?" (ESV). Just as a hammer can crush a rock, the Word of God can shatter false ideologies and any beliefs that aren't of Him. The Bible is powerful, and it will transform you.

Jesus said, "If you love me, you will keep my commandments" (John 14:15, ESV). In the same way, when we love God's Word, we are naturally drawn to live according to it—not because we have to but because we want to. Obeying His Word becomes a delight.

We don't read Scripture just to learn about God; He changes us as we study who He is. I once read that adoration of the Word also leads to adoration of the One who spoke it. As you read God's Word, the fire of first love begins to burn again, and you will start to live out David's words in Psalm 119:11, "I have hidden your word in my heart that I might not sin against you."

My heart has been burning to see people discipled, to teach them how to actually live out their faith, so I looked up statistics concerning the American church. Studies have shown that while a significant number of Americans identify as Christian and attend church regularly, a considerable number do not actively engage in discipleship.

The Barna Group found that while around 40 percent of Americans attend church services at least once a month, fewer actively engage in personal Bible study or prayer, which are key indicators of a committed faith.[2] Meanwhile, Pew Research found that while 75 percent of Christians attend church services, only about 20 percent are involved in small groups or Bible studies that foster deeper spiritual growth.[3] And the American Bible Society's *State of the Bible* report noted that while many Americans own a Bible and identify as Christian, only about 24 percent read it at least once a week outside of church.[4] These statistics explain why there is a gap between church attendance and genuine spiritual growth.

To walk in love, humility, forgiveness, and righteousness is to live like Christ. These are the traits that reflect His character. As I mentioned, Paul lists the fruit of the Spirit in Galatians 5:22–23. I challenge you to go through each one in that passage and consider whether it is evident in your life. Remember, real spiritual transformation is what threatens the devil's plans. That's why he loves it when Christians go to church but don't become people whose lives truly reflect Christ.

Ephesians 6:11–12 urges us to put on the full armor of God so we will be able to stand against the devil's schemes. It's time to move from routine to transformation. God is looking for heart change, which comes through surrendering to Him daily, being intentional about growing in relationship with Him, and staying committed to being a doer, not just a hearer, of the Word.

James 1:22 says, "Do not merely listen to the word, and so deceive yourselves. Do what it says." This means we can't just hear about Christlikeness; we must actively seek to become more like Him in our thoughts, words, and actions.

The devil is not afraid of our church attendance or conference participation, but he is deeply troubled when we seek to become more like Christ. It's time we move beyond temporary experiences and embrace a life of true transformation.

A man of God once told me, "Salvation is Jesus laying down His life for you; discipleship is you laying down your life for Him." Our challenge is to move beyond routine and allow the power of the Holy Spirit to change us from the inside out.

Is your life stormproof?

Take a moment to reflect on your own walk with God. Is there a difference between the faith you profess and the faith you live out? Are you going through the motions, or are you experiencing a heart-level transformation that reflects the character of Christ? Ask yourself, What areas of my life need to be fully surrendered to God for genuine change to happen?

Father, I come before You today acknowledging that I can't simply go through the motions. I don't want to live a life of routine Christianity but one that is truly transformed by Your love and power. Help me to examine my heart, and reveal where there is complacency or counterfeit faith. I surrender all that I am to You—my desires, my ambitions, and my comforts. May my life bear the fruit of true discipleship. I invite the power of Your Holy Spirit to do a deep work in me so that I may live a life that brings glory to Your name. In Jesus' name, amen.

CHAPTER 7

FAITH IN ACTION

WHILE MINISTERING AT a conference in Las Vegas, I had the opportunity to go riding on a utility terrain vehicle (UTV) with some friends in the desert of Nevada. It was an exciting adventure as each group of riders set off with their own tour guide.

As we rode, I soon found myself at the back of my group. At first I didn't think much of it, but it didn't take long to realize I was falling behind. The group ahead of me was moving fast, and no matter how hard I tried, I couldn't catch up.

As the dust thickened and the trail became harder to see, a wave of panic set in. I was lost in the desert and didn't know which way to go. To make matters worse, the paths ahead split in several directions, and I had no clue which one would lead me back to my group. I felt isolated and unsure what to do next.

Then, out of nowhere, I spotted a large cloud of dust rising in the distance. I immediately knew what it was. It was my group. I couldn't see them directly, but the cloud of dust they kicked up was clear evidence of their presence.

Without hesitation I turned in the direction of the dust cloud and followed it. A few minutes later I was back with my group, safe and sound.

But that wasn't the last time I fell behind. It happened again. Once more I lost track of the path and wondered where everyone had gone. But I again looked up and saw another cloud of dust rising in the desert. I followed it and soon caught up with my group.

That's when I felt the Lord speak to me and say, "Follow the cloud."

A Cloud in the Wilderness

My experience in the desert made me think of the Israelites' journey through the wilderness recorded in the Book of Exodus. When God led the Israelites out of Egypt, He didn't just give them instructions and send them off on their own. No, He led them with His presence in the form of a cloud by day and a pillar of fire by night.

> By day the LORD went ahead of them in a pillar of cloud to guide them on their way and by night in a pillar of fire to give them light, so that they could travel by day or night. Neither the pillar of cloud by day nor the pillar of fire by night left its place in front of the people.
>
> —EXODUS 13:21–22

This cloud wasn't just a visible sign of God's presence; it was a means of direction, protection, and assurance. When the cloud moved, they moved. When the cloud stopped, they stopped.

Friend, in the same way we cannot live without air, we have no spiritual life or direction without the presence of God! Just as He led the Israelites with the pillar of cloud, God desires to guide us on this narrow road of faith. The cloud didn't merely show them the way—it was the way. It went ahead of them, showing the path and ensuring they never lost direction. They didn't have to figure out the way or worry about getting lost; they simply followed the cloud.

Follow the Cloud, Not the Crowd

Psalm 119:105 tells us that God's Word is a lamp unto our feet and a light unto our path. And the Holy Spirit leads us into all truth (John 16:13). When we follow the Cloud of His presence, we can walk confidently, knowing we're in His will.

The beautiful truth is that the same cloud that surrounded the

Israelites dwells in you and me. The Holy Spirit is our Guide on this faith walk.

But today there's a constant tug-of-war between following the Cloud and following the crowd. The culture around us wants us to conform to its way of thinking and embrace its beliefs and ideologies. The crowd may offer temporary pleasure or approval, but it can never provide true peace.

You might wonder how to recognize the crowd in today's world. The crowd represents the popular path, the easy way. It's the broad road described in Matthew 7:13 that many are on but that leads to destruction. It is the path where social media, peer pressure, and cultural trends can drown out what a person knows is true according to God's Word.

The crowd today is found in voices that sow division, promote destruction, and ridicule those who disagree. I've noticed that wherever the image of God is being erased, the crowd isn't far behind. This is because the enemy, the god of this world, blinds minds and leads people astray.

> The god of this age has blinded the minds of unbelievers, so that they cannot see the light of the gospel that displays the glory of Christ, who is the image of God.
>
> —2 CORINTHIANS 4:4

This crowd embraces perversion and promotes ideas that directly oppose God's Word. These messages are everywhere—in movies, TV shows, and even schools. They don't even hide it anymore. These false, anti-Christ ideologies are leading many astray, particularly the younger generation.

Proverbs 14:12 warns, "There is a way that seems right to a man, but its end is the way to death" (ESV). But there is another way—a narrow road that leads to life. The way to walk this road is by following the Cloud of God's presence.

Psalm 1:1–6 reminds us of the joy that comes to those who avoid the advice of the wicked and instead delight in God's Word, meditating on it day and night. Such people are like trees planted by streams of water, always bearing fruit and prospering in all they do.

I searched the Scriptures for examples of what happened to those who followed the crowd instead of God, and here's what I found:

- In the days of Noah, the crowd perished, and only eight people survived (Gen. 7:13, 21–23).

- After the flood, the crowd defied God by building the Tower of Babel in an attempt to make a name for themselves (Gen. 11:1–9).

- In Abraham's time, the crowd turned to idol worship, even Abraham's own family (Josh. 24:2).

- In Moses' time, the crowd worshipped the golden calf (Exod. 32).

- When Joshua and Caleb went to spy out the Promised Land, the crowd doubted God's promise and cowered in fear (Num. 13–14).

- In the wilderness, the Israelites who doubted God died without entering the Promised Land (Num. 14:29–32; Heb. 3:17–19; 1 Cor. 10:5).

- In Samuel's time, the crowd in Israel wanted a king to be like the other nations (1 Sam. 8:4–7).

- In Saul's time, the entire Israelite army was afraid of the giant Goliath, but one young man, David, stood up to him (1 Sam. 17).

- In Elijah's day, 450 prophets of Baal called on their god, and only one prophet of the Lord stood against them (1 Kings 18). But God was with the one!

- In Daniel's time, the crowd bowed to Nebuchadnezzar's golden statue; three men stood firm, and God delivered them from death (Dan. 3).

- Jesus warned that the crowd is on the road to destruction while those who follow the narrow path—the Cloud—are on their way to eternal life (Matt. 7:13–14).

- It was the crowd that yelled, "Crucify him!" (Matt. 27:22–23).

Even today, Jesus calls us to step away from the crowd and follow Him.

You don't have to be part of the crowd anymore. You don't have to sit quietly, agreeing with everything around you, pretending to fit in. Jesus is calling you to step away from the crowd and follow Him!

Too often we Christians get caught up in what the crowd is doing. We talk about the same things, follow the same trends, and get swept along by their agenda. But Jesus isn't asking us to blend in. He's inviting us to follow Him. It was in the cloud that Jesus ascended (Acts 1:9), and it is on a cloud that Jesus will return (Mark 13:26). He's the One who matters. We must seek His presence, Spirit, and truth.

Following Jesus on His Terms

Jesus says in John 6:53, "Unless you eat the flesh of the Son of Man and drink his blood, you have no life in you." In John chapter 6, thousands of people had followed Jesus after witnessing the miraculous feeding of the five thousand. They were drawn by the excitement, the miracles, and perhaps even the hope of another free meal. But when Jesus began to speak about eating His flesh and drinking His blood, the atmosphere shifted.

The same crowd that had clamored for His attention now turned away. Why? The moment following Him no longer served their selfish desires, they decided it wasn't worth it. They weren't ready for the deeper commitment Jesus required.

Many of us today can identify with that crowd. We come to Jesus seeking blessings, healing, or solutions to our problems. But when His words challenge us or make us uncomfortable, we're tempted to pull back. We want things to go our way. Well, Jesus isn't interested in followers who seek Him only for what they can gain. He is calling us to something much deeper.

Jesus isn't asking us to blend in. He's inviting us to follow Him.

The challenge for the crowd—and for us—is to move beyond satisfying our immediate desires and recognize the need for spiritual sustenance. Many walked away when they realized following Jesus meant accepting hard truths and making a commitment to live out their faith. Jesus was asking them (and us) to consider: Do we follow Him for what He can give us, or for who He is?

In a moment of clarity Peter said, "Lord, to whom shall we go? You have the words of eternal life" (John 6:68). His heart was gripped, and he understood what the crowd didn't—that true life is found in Christ alone. When we choose to follow Jesus, we must do it on His terms, not ours.

What does it mean to follow Jesus on His terms? It means embracing the messages that cut through our hearts and responding to the call to sacrifice. Jesus calls us to a relationship that is transformative, one that requires us to lay down our own agendas and desires.

Consider your own life. Are you following Jesus for what He can do for you, or for who He is? Are you drawn to the miracles, the popular preachers, and the blessings, or are you truly committed to living out His Word, even when it convicts and stretches you?

This kind of faith requires moving beyond a transactional relationship with God—one where we approach Him only when it serves our purposes.

Take another moment to reflect. Are there areas where you've followed Jesus on your own terms? Have there been times when you turned away because His words or the uncompromising message of the gospel felt too challenging?

How can we change if we are not challenged? Jesus desires followers who will stay with Him, not just for the miracles but because they recognize that He alone has the words of eternal life!

Following God When It's Inconvenient

It's easy to talk about following God when things are smooth and doors swing wide open. We love when God blesses us with favor or new opportunities. But what about when His presence leads us into uncomfortable, inconvenient, or even difficult places?

Following the Cloud isn't always about walking through open doors. Sometimes it's about following God's prompting to step into tough situations: forgiving when it's difficult, speaking truth when it's uncomfortable, or going out of your way to bless someone in need.

A few years ago, a pastor friend asked me to help him move into his new home. I drove from Chicago to Wisconsin, ready to spend the day helping him. On the way, I noticed I only had about a quarter tank of gas but figured it would be enough. I was on the freeway, thirty minutes from my destination, when the fuel light came on.

I began praying, asking God to help me make it to a gas station. Eventually, I saw an exit with a few stations. As I prepared to pull off, I felt the Lord say, "Go to the one on the right, and look for a man in a yellow jacket. Give him $50 and tell him I love him."

I immediately thought, "This can't be God. I only have $37 in my wallet, and it's almost 100 degrees outside. No one is wearing a jacket." But as I pulled up to the gas station on the right, I couldn't shake the feeling. I began filling up my tank, looking around for someone in a yellow jacket. Everyone I saw was dressed in summer clothes.

I walked to the front of the gas station and stood there for about 45 seconds, trying to make sense of what I'd heard in my heart. Then, out of nowhere, a motorcycle pulled up right in front of me. The rider was wearing a jacket with yellow stripes. My heart sank. It was exactly what God had shown me.

I was nervous, but I couldn't ignore the prompting, so I walked up to the man. "Sir," I said, "this might sound crazy, but when I pulled up, I felt like God told me that there would be someone here wearing a yellow jacket and I needed to tell you how much He loves you."

The man's eyes filled with tears. He explained he was from North Carolina, riding 10,000 miles to raise awareness for men's mental health and addiction. He had been feeling discouraged, wondering if his efforts were making a difference.

He went on to share that he had been a pastor for twenty years. In that moment, the Holy Spirit reminded me to bless him financially.

I thought, "Lord, I only have $37, not $50." But I felt like God was saying, "Go inside, withdraw the money from the ATM, and give it to him." So I told the man, "I'll be right back." I went inside and withdrew the cash. As I handed it to him, I said, "I just felt led to give this to you and say that God is so proud of you."

The man broke down in tears and hugged me. He told me that the word was incredibly timely and that every dollar raised went directly to charity.

That moment reminded me of the importance of stepping out in faith, listening to the Holy Spirit, and responding—even when it's inconvenient. By following God's presence and trusting His direction, I was able to bless someone in need.

DIVINE APPOINTMENTS

I believe God gives us multiple divine appointments every single day. He is always setting up opportunities for us to share the gospel, pray for someone, or plant a seed of encouragement. We can miss these moments if we're not looking for them. But when we do pay attention to the Holy Spirit's promptings, even the briefest encounter can become a life-changing moment for someone.

That's what happened to me at the gas station with the man in the yellow jacket. I could have ignored the prompting. It seemed random, awkward, and even a little strange. But by choosing to act on the tug I felt in my spirit, I spoke life into someone who needed it, encouraged him, and even blessed him financially.

Are you following Jesus for what He can do for you, or for who He is?

The reality is, many people want to follow God when it's convenient, but few are willing to follow Him into the hard stuff—when it costs them something and they have to overcome their fears and move without hesitation. Most Christians are eager for God to lead them into prosperity or breakthrough, but will we follow when He leads us to forgive someone who's hurt us deeply or to speak the truth in a difficult conversation, even if it makes things awkward or uncomfortable?

It's easy to say "I'll follow God's presence" when it leads to a promotion, a new ministry opportunity, or a new season of blessing. But will we follow when He calls us to love those who are difficult to love or to step into someone else's mess to help serve them?

This is where faith is tested. Faith in action isn't convenient; it's transformative. It's easy to follow when things are going great, but the mark of true obedience is being willing to follow God when it's hard, when His prompting doesn't make sense and the sacrifice feels real.

So ask yourself, Am I ready to follow the Cloud, not just when it's leading me to blessings and new opportunities but also into the hard and uncomfortable places where true growth happens?

How to Move with the Cloud

Much like my experience in the desert, some seasons in life can leave us feeling lost. We move forward, full of excitement and purpose, only to find ourselves falling behind, confused, or unsure which path to take. We may see others moving ahead and wonder if we've missed something or strayed off course.

In those moments we must remember the lesson I learned in the desert: Follow the Cloud.

Just as God's presence, in the form of a visible cloud, guided the Israelites through the wilderness to the Promised Land, He will guide us too. We are called to follow God's presence. But how does this look in our daily lives? Here's how we can follow the Cloud practically:

1. Look for the Cloud of God's presence. In the desert, I had to look up and spot the cloud of dust in the distance to find my group. In the same way, we must train our spiritual eyes to seek God's guidance.

While we may not see a literal cloud or pillar of fire, God speaks to us through His Word, prayer, the Holy Spirit, and other believers. When you feel lost or unsure, look up—seek signs of His presence and follow them.

2. Trust the Cloud when you're lost. In the desert, when I felt lost and uncertain, seeing the cloud gave me a sense of direction and reassurance. In life, when we feel like we're losing our way—whether in relationships, work, ministry, or our spiritual walk—we need to look for God's guidance.

God's presence will never leave us. As I followed that dust cloud,

I didn't question whether it would lead me to my group. I trusted that it would guide me where I needed to go. The same is true spiritually. When we follow God's presence, we can trust that He will guide us to where we need to be.

3. Be willing to follow even when you can't see the whole picture. One of the hardest parts of following the cloud in the desert was that I couldn't see where it was leading me. I had to follow without knowing the full path.

The same is true when God leads us. He doesn't always show us the entire plan or provide every detail. Instead, He calls us to trust and follow Him step by step. The Israelites didn't know the exact route through the wilderness, but they trusted the cloud was leading them to the Promised Land.

4. Follow the Cloud until you're back with the group. When I felt lost in the desert, following the cloud always brought me back to my group. Similarly, when we follow God's presence, He brings us back to where we need to be—whether that's in fellowship with Him or with others.

We are never truly alone. The Holy Spirit is always with us, leading us into all truth.

The next time you feel lost, as I did in the desert, remember to follow the Cloud. Trust that God's presence is always with you, guiding you and leading you back to the right path.

I was never truly lost as long as I had the cloud to follow. And you are never truly lost when you have God's presence to guide you.

So look up. Seek God's presence. Trust His guidance. Follow the Cloud, and you will always find your way.

Is your life stormproof?

Are you truly following God's presence, or are you just following the crowd? Are you following God only when it's convenient, or are you willing to trust Him when it's hard? When it feels like everyone else is going a different way? When it costs you something?

It's easy to get caught up in the noise around us—the opinions, trends, and quick fixes. But God isn't in the crowd. He's in the Cloud.

> *Lord, thank You for Your constant presence in my life. Help me keep my eyes fixed on You, even when the path seems uncertain. Teach me to recognize the Cloud of Your presence in every situation, and give me the courage to follow it, even when it takes me into unknown or difficult places. May I not be swayed by the crowd but instead walk faithfully with You. I trust that You are guiding me toward Your purpose, and I surrender my own plans to follow You on Your terms. In Jesus' name, amen.*

CHAPTER 8

FUEL YOUR FAITH

RECENTLY, I ORDERED some vitamins to help strengthen my immune system because I travel frequently. I know that to stay healthy and fight off sickness, my body needs the right kind of support—vitamins, minerals, and nutrients that boost my immune health. It's a simple thing, but the day these vitamins arrived, I started reflecting on how just as our physical bodies need nourishment to stay strong, our spiritual lives need the right kind of "fuel" to remain healthy.

In the same way that I take vitamins to support my immune system, there's something we can do spiritually to strengthen our hearts and souls. That "fuel" for our spiritual lives is prayer.

Prayer is like vitamins for our spirit. In the same way our immune system depends on nutrients to fight off illness, our spiritual life needs prayer to combat weakness, temptation, and complacency.

When I ordered those vitamins, it wasn't because I was already sick but because I wanted to avoid getting sick. I know that if I consistently take care of my body and give it the right nutrients, it will be stronger and better prepared to fight off sickness.

The same is true spiritually. We face battles every day—temptations, discouragement, trials, and lies from the enemy that can weaken our faith. The devil seeks to attack our hearts and minds, and if we're not careful, our spiritual "immunity" can run low.

The apostle Paul understood the importance of spiritual strength, which is why he urged the church in Ephesians 6:10–11, "Finally, be strong in the Lord and in his mighty power. Put on the full armor of God, so that you can take your stand against the devil's schemes."

Just as we don't wait until we're physically sick to start supporting our immune system, we shouldn't wait until we're spiritually weak to strengthen ourselves in the Lord. We need to regularly nourish our spirit through prayer so we will be prepared for whatever storms come our way.

Our souls are designed to connect with God daily. The psalmist writes in Psalm 42:1, "As the deer pants for streams of water, so my soul pants for you, my God." As a deer longs for water to survive, our souls crave daily, genuine encounters with the living God. Prayer is the stream that refreshes and sustains us.

When we neglect prayer, it's like denying our souls the nourishment they need. Over time we start to feel restless and empty and begin seeking peace and satisfaction in other things or people—things that can never truly fill the void.

Every day we face a choice: to strengthen our relationship with God or to neglect it; to feed our spirit or feed our flesh. Galatians 6:8 teaches us, "Whoever sows to please their flesh, from the flesh will reap destruction; whoever sows to please the Spirit, from the Spirit will reap eternal life." What we choose to focus on each day has a direct impact on our spiritual growth.

Think of your spirit like a garden. Whatever you feed it will grow. If you consistently nurture your spirit with prayer, Scripture, and worship, it will flourish, and you'll experience spiritual growth. But if you neglect it, turning your attention to distractions or worldly pursuits, your spirit can wither. Skipping prayer is like denying your spirit the nourishment it needs. If you find yourself feeling on edge, ask yourself, When was the last time I spent quality time in God's presence?

Prayer is what strengthens our spirit, brings clarity, and renews our appetite for the things of God. In the same way we don't just take vitamins when we're already sick, we don't just pray when we're facing a crisis. We should be praying regularly to keep our spiritual immune system strong so we're prepared for life's storms.

If you took vitamins only occasionally, they wouldn't have much of an effect. Similarly, if we pray only in moments of desperation, we may find ourselves spiritually weak and unprepared for life's challenges. But when we prioritize prayer as a regular part of our lives, we build a strong spiritual foundation that equips us to face trials with faith and confidence.

The Power of Regular Prayer: Building Immunity

I find it amazing how the physical world often parallels God's design for the spiritual world. Whether it's personal hygiene or fueling our cars, when we neglect proper maintenance, things fail to operate as intended. Consider the following examples.

Handwashing—Think about how essential it is to wash your hands regularly. If we neglect this simple act, germs build up, leading to sickness. In the same way, daily spiritual practices like prayer and repentance cleanse our hearts and keep us spiritually healthy. James 4:8 says, "Come near to God and he will come near to you. Wash your hands, you sinners, and purify your hearts, you double-minded." In the same way handwashing removes physical dirt and contaminants, regular prayer and repentance remove spiritual "germs" that weigh us down.

Fueling a car—A car won't run without fuel, no matter how well it's built. In the same way, our spiritual lives need regular nourishment from God's Word. Jesus says in Matthew 4:4, "Man shall not live on bread alone, but on every word that comes from the mouth of God." The Bible is the fuel that sustains and empowers our faith.

Brushing your teeth—Neglecting to brush your teeth leads to a buildup of plaque and eventually decay. In the same way, neglecting your relationship with God can lead to spiritual decay! Proverbs 4:23 says, "Above all else, guard your heart, for everything you do flows from it." Spending time in prayer and in God's Word each day helps us guard our hearts and remain spiritually healthy, much like brushing our teeth protects against decay.

If you look, you can see God's handiwork in everything. Even these seemingly mundane aspects of life can remind us of our need for God. Genesis 1 shows us that God created the world with purpose. Every aspect of creation reflects His intentional design.

In fact, take a moment and look around. Have you ever noticed how everything in nature seems to reach upward, as if pointing to God? Every blade of grass standing tall and reaching for the sky is a silent testimony. How powerful is that? It's as if the grass knows where it comes from and where it belongs. Each blade points to heaven.

When we neglect prayer, it's like denying our souls the nourishment they need.

Psalm 19:1 says, "The heavens declare the glory of God; the skies proclaim the work of his hands." Everything around us, from the tiniest blade of grass to the tallest mountain, is constantly pointing to God. Look at a tree. Its branches stretch up, reaching for the sun and reminding us that everything longs for the Son of God!

Everything around us points toward God. The mountains, the trees, and even the grass beneath our feet remind us of where we come from and where we're headed—back to our Creator!

So when you see a tree reaching toward the sky or a blade of grass standing tall, let it be a reminder to you that everything in creation is pointing to the One who made it all. And we too are made to reach toward God in worship and surrender, for He is the source of life.

The world functions because of the way God designed it, and our lives function best when we come into alignment with God's purpose. Paul says in 1 Corinthians 14:40, "But everything should be done in a fitting and orderly way." Living our lives according to God's Word helps us live effectively and with purpose.

ASCENDING THE HILL OF THE LORD

One day I was at my studio trying to pray. Fifty minutes in, I was still struggling to connect with God. My flesh kept pestering me to leave and get something to eat, while the enemy relentlessly reminded me of my past mistakes. It felt like the devil was throwing every distraction at me to keep me from entering into that place of prayer.

Frustrated, I stood up, ready to give up. But then I remembered something pastor Jentezen Franklin of Free Chapel in Gainesville, Georgia, had said in a sermon: "If you can't hear God, read God." I grabbed my Bible from the table, determined to push through. I also recalled my dad's advice from when I was growing up: "Read a proverb a day. There's so much wisdom in it." Taking his words to heart, I decided to read Proverbs for a while.

I opened to chapter 13 and quickly found a verse that convicted me: "He who guards his mouth preserves his life, but he who opens wide his lips shall have destruction" (v. 3, NKJV). I paused, letting the words sink in, and asked myself, Have there been moments in my life when I could've avoided drama or pain if I'd just guarded my mouth?

Next, I flipped to the Psalms and started reading wherever my eyes landed. Psalm 24:3–6 jumped out at me:

> Who may ascend the mountain of the LORD? Who may stand in his holy place? The one who has clean hands and a pure heart, who does not trust in an idol or swear by a false god. They will receive blessing from the LORD and vindication from God their Savior. Such is the generation of those who seek him, who seek your face, God of Jacob.

As I read, conviction gripped me. I closed my Bible and began to repent—not just for the times I hadn't guarded my mouth but also for the sins I might not even have been aware of.

In that moment I realized I was doing exactly what the psalm described: "cleaning" my hands and "purifying" my heart. And as I prayed, something shifted. I felt myself rising above the surface-level concerns that had been distracting me and ascending to a more intimate place with God.

Psalm 24 begins with a powerful question: "Who may ascend the mountain of the LORD?" The mountain represents a higher place—a place closer to God. Ascending it requires effort, perseverance, and a deep desire to draw near to Him. God longs for us to come close, as James 4:8 tells us, "Draw near to God and He will draw near to you" (NKJV).

GETTING PAST THE FLESH

When you first start praying, it's common to feel distracted, tired, or overwhelmed by thoughts. This is your flesh pulling you back into the worries and cares of everyday life. Romans 7:18 explains, "Nothing good dwells in me, that is, in my flesh" (NASB). Pushing past these distractions takes intentional effort. As my evangelist friend David Diga Hernandez often says, prayer is the death of the flesh.

The flesh represents our human tendencies—doubt, fear, distraction, impatience, and the desire for comfort. We're naturally wired to seek pleasure and avoid pain. Galatians 5:17 explains this ongoing struggle: "For the flesh desires what is contrary to the Spirit, and the Spirit what is contrary to the flesh. They are in conflict with each other, so that you are not to do whatever you want."

To win this battle, we must first recognize it. Become aware of your weaknesses and the areas where you tend to fail. Then, learn to put your flesh under subjection. This means making a daily decision to put to death what is earthly in us and follow Jesus. This isn't a one-time fix; it's a continual commitment to choose God over self.

This struggle can make prayer hard, but we cannot subdue the flesh in our own strength. We need the Holy Spirit to empower us to resist the temptations of the flesh. As you persist in prayer, pushing through the distractions and discomfort, you'll begin to experience a shift. You'll rise above the noise of everyday life and experience a deeper connection with God.

PRAY UNTIL YOU ASCEND

The key to breakthrough in prayer is to keep praying until you ascend. As you push through, you move past the surface-level worries and distractions to enter a place where you can truly hear God and feel His presence. This is where you experience the "fullness of joy" that comes from being in God's manifest presence (Ps. 16:11, MEV).

One of the signs that you've ascended is when you begin to pray with authority and confidence. Luke 10:19 reminds us that we've been given authority to overcome obstacles: "I have given you authority to trample on snakes and scorpions and to overcome all the power of the enemy; nothing will harm you."

When you are in tune with God, your prayers become powerful and effective. Unfortunately, too many people never reach this place because they settle for surface-level prayer or give up too soon.

To experience this deeper state of prayer, you must persevere. Push past the resistance of the flesh until you fully enter God's presence. It's in this sacred place of deep communion with Him that you begin to see answers to your prayers and experience shifts in your circumstances or mindset.

James 5:16 says, "The prayer of a righteous person is powerful and effective." God wants every believer to reach this place where transformation happens—not just in your circumstances but in your heart. To get there, you must forget about the clock and truly seek Him.

Jeremiah 29:13 promises, "You will seek me and find me when you seek me with all your heart." This kind of wholehearted pursuit not only causes us to ascend but also leads to spiritual growth and a deeper relationship with God.

Don't neglect the discipline of daily prayer. Build an altar where you can meet with God each day. The Hebrew word for *altar* means "a place of surrender." It's the place where you bring your burdens and let go of your idols. It's a place of exchange where sacrifice happens—a private, sacred space for encounters with God.

Many people ask God to send the fire of His presence, but He is looking for a place to pour it out. I've learned that God always sends the fire on a sacrifice. When we place ourselves on the altar in complete surrender, He will send the fire. His presence will consume everything we've laid down before Him.

REQUIREMENTS FOR ASCENDING

Again, Psalm 24:3–4 asks, "Who may ascend the mountain of the LORD? Who may stand in his holy place? The one who has clean hands and a pure heart, who does not trust in an idol or swear by a false god." In these verses, we see there are requirements for ascending the hill of the Lord. We must have the following:

- **Clean hands**—This represents our actions. Are we living in a way that truly honors God? This is where we need to examine ourselves. Are our daily choices reflecting His will?

- **A pure heart**—Our intentions matter. In Matthew 5:8 Jesus says, "Blessed are the pure in heart, for they will see God." A pure heart means having a deep reverence for God and a sincere desire to follow His ways.

- **No trust in idols**—An idol is anything we love, fear, or trust more than Jesus. Anything that takes priority over God in our hearts is an idol. And if you have an idol, that means you have a "lesser lover" in your life. Anything that takes priority over Jesus is a lesser lover. In Matthew 6:21 Jesus says, "For where your treasure is, there your heart will be also." This verse reminds us that our hearts follow what we value most.

> If we value someone or something more than our
> relationship with Jesus, we allow that person or thing
> to take His place in our hearts.

You may be wondering how you can identify these lesser lovers. Think about what you spend the most time on. If you're giving more time to something than you're giving to prayer and reading God's Word, it's a sign that thing might be taking the top spot in your life.

Also consider what you worry about most. Our anxieties reveal what really has our attention. If your mind is consumed with cares, the things you're worried about may have become your lesser lovers.

Finally, ask yourself, What do I daydream about? Pay attention to where your thoughts go. If your mind drifts to things other than Jesus, it's time for a heart check. Lesser lovers always come at a cost. They will never truly satisfy your soul. As we saw earlier, in John 4 Jesus talks to the woman at the well, pointing out how she's been searching for fulfillment in relationships. He tells her that true satisfaction only comes from Him—the living water.

Our hearts are meant to be filled by Jesus alone. These requirements for ascending are meant to help us grow in our relationship with God and get rid of lesser lovers. The Lord wants us to come to Him honestly and authentically, free from distractions and the things that weigh us down.

The secret place is where we meet with God. It's that quiet, personal space where we can experience Him and build history with Him. It's where we surrender and come under His lordship.

When we spend time in prayer, we are not only growing in our relationship with Jesus; we are also weakening our flesh. When we skip prayer, we begin to drift away from God's presence, just as a boat drifts without an anchor.

Hebrews 2:1 warns us, "We must pay the most careful attention, therefore, to what we have heard, so that we do not drift away." Missing appointments with God in the secret place makes it harder to stay close to Him. It affects our demeanor toward others and causes us to become more easily irritated and impatient.

THE REWARDS OF ASCENDING

When we follow those requirements and ascend the hill of the Lord, rewards will be waiting for us. These include the following:

- **Blessing**—Psalm 24:5 says those who ascend the hill of the Lord will receive blessings from the Lord. These blessings aren't just material; they're also spiritual benefits such as peace, joy, understanding, and a stronger awareness of God's presence in your life.

- **Vindication**—God will affirm and validate those who draw near to Him. In Matthew 6:6 Jesus says, "When you pray, go into your room, close the door and pray to your Father, who is unseen. Then your Father, who sees what is done in secret, will reward you." This reward is a form of vindication.

- **Transformation**—In the secret place, we are changed. That's the main byproduct of being in God's presence. Second Corinthians 3:18 says, "And we all, who with unveiled faces contemplate the Lord's glory, are being transformed into his image with ever-increasing glory." The more we behold Him, the more we become like Him.

Ascending the hill of the Lord is really an invitation to intimacy, transformation, and blessing. It requires time, effort, honesty, and a deep desire to pursue God above everything else. But getting close to God is worth whatever it costs us, because when we draw near to Him, we experience His presence and the fullness of joy and peace only He can give.

RECOGNIZING JESUS

In Luke 24 we find two disciples walking down the road to Emmaus. Their hearts were heavy, burdened with the recent events of Jesus' crucifixion. As they talked about everything that had happened in the past few days, they didn't recognize Jesus as He walked alongside them.

Everything changed, however, when they invited Him to stay with them. In the breaking of the bread their eyes were opened, and they recognized Him. As I was reading this passage one morning during my devotion time, the Holy Spirit showed me something profound about communion with Jesus.

Ascending the hill of the Lord is an invitation to intimacy, transformation, and blessing.

We see in Luke 24:15–16 that "Jesus Himself drew near and went with them," but "their eyes were kept from recognizing Him" (MEV). There's a twofold message here. First, God wanted the disciples to invite Him in. He doesn't force Himself into our lives—He waits for an invitation, working in cooperation with our free will.

Second, this passage shows that even when Jesus is walking with us, we can fail to see Him if our vision is clouded by life's storms, confusion, or disappointment. Many of us are walking through our own version of the road to Emmaus, unaware that the Savior is right beside us.

But as Jesus walked with those disciples, He walks with us, even in the hardest seasons of life. The truth is, God is nearer to us than we think. All He asks is that we invite Him into our difficult moments and let Him reveal Himself as the God of breakthrough.

As the day ended in Luke 24, the disciples extended an invitation to Jesus, asking Him to stay with them, even though they didn't fully understand who He was. This invitation is key. As I mentioned, Jesus doesn't force Himself into our lives. He waits for us to open the door.

Jesus says in Revelation 3:20, "Here I am! I stand at the door and knock. If anyone hears my voice and opens the door, I will come in and eat with that person, and they with me." When we invite Him in, He manifests His presence and begins to open our eyes to the truth of who He is.

RECOGNIZING JESUS IN THE BREAKING OF BREAD

The revelation comes in Luke 24:30–31: "When he was at table with them, he took the bread and blessed and broke it and gave it to them. And their eyes were opened, and they recognized him" (ESV).

This moment is profound. The act of breaking bread is more than just sharing a meal—it represents communion with Jesus. It's a reminder of His body, broken on the cross to save us from our sins, and the power of His resurrection.

As these disciples recognized Jesus in the breaking of the bread, we too can recognize Him when we understand the significance of His broken body. It's in this revelation that our eyes are opened and we see Him for who He truly is.

Jesus didn't just break the bread so the disciples could see Him. He broke it so they could understand His sacrifice. How great is our God that His body was broken so ours might be made whole. His blood was poured out so we might be forgiven and restored.

After they recognized Jesus, the disciples said, "Did not our hearts burn within us while he talked to us on the road, while he opened to us the Scriptures?" (Luke 24:32, ESV). Recognizing Jesus ignites in our hearts a fresh passion for Him and a renewed desire to follow Him.

GROWING IN CHRIST CHANGES YOUR APPETITE

As we get older, our desires and values naturally change. What once seemed important often loses its appeal as we begin to focus on what truly matters. For example, the things I wanted when I was twenty-one no longer hold the same appeal. My values and priorities have shifted.

The same thing happens in our spiritual lives. Just as maturity changes our earthly appetites, growing in Christ transforms our spiritual appetites. The apostle Paul says in 1 Corinthians 13:11, "When I was a child, I talked like a child, I thought like a child, I reasoned like a child. When I became a man, I put the ways of childhood behind me."

As we grow in Christ, our appetite for sin fades and we develop a hunger for holiness. We begin to desire what pleases the Lord and avoid what hinders our fellowship with Him.

Mature Christians pursue righteousness and holiness. Second Timothy 2:22 encourages us, "Flee the evil desires of youth and pursue righteousness, faith, love and peace, along with those who call on the Lord out of a pure heart."

In the same way aging in the natural shifts our earthly appetites, growing in Christ changes our spiritual appetites. Our goals and priorities shift, and we begin to value the things that feed our spirit more than the things that feed our flesh.

STAYING SPIRITUALLY HEALTHY

To give God our best, we must prioritize our time with Him. Discover the time of day when you're most focused and energetic, and build a routine around it to make prayer a priority.

When we pray, the Holy Spirit strengthens us, and His power flows through us. Remember the analogy of the vitamins I ordered? Just as they help the body fight off sickness, prayer helps us fight off the attacks of the enemy and the weariness that comes from life's storms. In the same way we feel stronger and more energized when we take care of our bodies, we become more spiritually alert when we stay connected to the power source—Jesus.

Don't wait until you're spiritually "sick" or overwhelmed to pray. Make prayer a regular part of your life today, just like taking your daily vitamins. When you do, you'll notice your spiritual immune system getting stronger, and you'll be ready to face whatever storms come your way.

Is your life stormproof?

Are you making regular time for prayer, or are you waiting for a crisis to drive you to your knees? When was the last time you had a real, uninterrupted time of prayer? Have you been fueling your spirit or letting distractions take over? What changes do you need to make today to strengthen your spiritual immunity before the storms come?

> *Father, thank You for the daily opportunity to draw near to You. I know I can't make it through the battles of life on my own, and I recognize that my spiritual health depends on staying connected to You through prayer. I ask for Your help in making prayer a regular part of my life, not just when I'm struggling, but every day. Strengthen my spirit so I can face whatever comes my way. Help me to guard my heart, to keep my gaze on You above all else, and to strengthen my spirit in Your presence. Thank You for Your faithfulness and for being my source of strength. In Jesus' name, amen.*

CHAPTER 9

TRUST THE PROCESS

WHILE PRAYING IN my car one day, I had a vision. In this vision I was on a train, heading toward a destination. At first everything felt secure. The conductor, someone I trusted, was in charge, and I knew the train would take me to where I needed to go—on schedule, with certainty. But as time passed, I began to grow impatient. The stops seemed to come too slowly, and my frustration grew. I started to think maybe I could take control, find a shortcut, or get off and find a faster route. And so I did. I got off at a stop that wasn't mine. It wasn't part of the plan.

In that moment, God was showing me how many of us do the same thing. We get frustrated and impatient, and we step off the course God has set for us. How many times have we been there? We grow tired of waiting for God's timing, so we try to "reroute" the journey. We leave the path He set before us and end up at a destination that was never meant for us—all because we couldn't trust the process.

THE STRUGGLE TO WAIT

Waiting is hard. We live in a world that values speed, overnight success, and results on our terms. While we're waiting on God's timing, it can feel like He's forgotten about us. But the truth is, God's timing isn't slow—it's perfect. He is never late or early; He is always on time. We just get impatient.

One day, while waiting for my luggage at baggage claim, I felt

God speak to me. I had just gotten off the plane and was heading to ground transportation to grab my bag and meet my dad outside. I've never liked waiting for luggage—it always feels like an eternity. This time, after waiting a while, I texted my dad to pull up, thinking my bag would be out any second. I was impatient and thought I could save time. But when he pulled up, my bag still hadn't arrived. He had to circle around and wait for me to be ready.

Frustrated, I decided to ask at the airline office why it was taking so long. But just as I turned to leave, I looked back and saw my bag coming down the conveyor belt. The moment I almost gave up on waiting, there it was.

In that moment, God reminded me that when we're tempted to give up or take matters into our own hands, our breakthrough could be just around the corner. It was a lesson in patience and trust: Don't stop waiting on the Lord. It may take longer than we expect, but He knows exactly what He's doing.

Many of us are waiting for something we long for—whether it's a relationship, marriage, a breakthrough, or a dream we've held for years. And to be honest, it often feels like God has either forgotten or is simply not answering.

But what if God didn't forget? What if He's waiting for us to shift our focus, to find our deepest satisfaction in Him rather than in the things we want? What if, because of how much He loves us, He's withholding what we desire until we truly don't want it anymore? What if He does this not because He doesn't want us to have it but because He knows that only when we are fully satisfied in Him can we truly receive what He has for us?

We all have desires, and I believe these desires come from God. I once heard a man of God say, "God puts desire in us for what He desires for us." I've learned that the problem isn't desiring things— it's when we desire them more than we desire God. When our hearts are consumed by something else—whether it's success, relationships, or ministry—it becomes easy to make those desires idols.

We think about them constantly, seeking them first rather than seeking God first.

Jesus said in Matthew 6:33, "But seek first the kingdom of God and His righteousness, and all these things shall be added to you" (NKJV). Notice He didn't say, "Seek first your desires, and everything else will be added unto you." Instead, He said, "Seek first the kingdom of God." When we seek Him first, He purifies our desires to align with His will. He knows nothing can satisfy us like He can. When we fix our gaze on Him and make Him our true desire, everything else falls into place.

God's Timing and Withholding

Most of the time, God withholds what we want because we're not yet ready for it. It's not that He doesn't want us to be blessed; it's because He's protecting us. God knows whether we're prepared to handle the things we desire. The delay is about making sure our character matches our purpose.

In the waiting, God refines us. He teaches us to trust Him and to find contentment in Him alone. This is so important in waiting seasons. I've discovered that when God hasn't answered our prayers yet, He's preparing us to receive His blessings at the right time and in the right way. It's not just about the answer to the prayer—it's about what we learn while waiting for it.

Remember Isaiah 55:8–9: "For my thoughts are not your thoughts, neither are your ways my ways....As the heavens are higher than the earth, so are my ways higher than your ways and my thoughts than your thoughts."

As God withholds what we deeply desire, our hearts begin to shift. Over time our craving for the thing we wanted fades as we discover something greater: His presence. When we experience the fire of first love in our hearts, our desires become secondary to our devotion to Him. We realize He is enough.

This doesn't mean our desires disappear. It means they are now in their rightful place. Psalm 37:4 says, "Delight yourself also in the LORD, and He shall give you the desires of your heart" (NKJV). A great man of God once said, "When you delight yourself in the Lord, He doesn't give you what you want—He gives you what to want." That's a powerful truth!

James 1:17 says, "Every good gift and every perfect gift is from above, and comes down from the Father of lights, with whom there is no variation or shadow of turning" (NKJV). When God finally gives us the desires of our hearts, it will be according to His will, at His perfect time, and it will exceed our expectations!

THE CONSEQUENCES OF IMPATIENCE

When we step off the train before God has brought us to the right stop, we risk more than just delaying the journey—we miss out on everything God wants to teach us. Like a GPS rerouting, we may feel like we've found another way, but in reality we've only delayed our arrival at the destination God had in mind all along. Then we get frustrated, confused, and maybe even angry because it feels like God is taking too long.

> Most of the time, God withholds what we want because we're not yet ready for it.

God is always working, even in the waiting. Psalm 27:14 tells us, "Wait for the LORD; be strong and take heart and wait for the LORD." Waiting is an act of faith. It's saying we trust God more than what we currently see.

I remember hearing Bible teacher John Bevere say that complaining kept the Israelites from entering the Promised Land, and it can prevent us from entering ours as well.

God's will for us is perfect, and He has a plan for every season. Ecclesiastes 3:1 says, "There is a time for everything, and a season for every activity under the heavens." We need to trust that He knows exactly what He's doing. There are things He wants to do in us during the waiting seasons. If we take matters into our own hands, we risk missing out on these vital moments of preparation. Looking back, I'm grateful God didn't give me what I was praying for at the time because now I see how He was protecting me from things I didn't understand.

Staying on track teaches us patience, perseverance, and to trust in God's plan. God knows what He's doing, even when we don't. The journey isn't just about the destination—it's about the transformation that happens in us along the way. Through refinement, people will be able to see Jesus more clearly in us.

God is the Potter, and we are the clay. He wants to shape us into something beautiful. In waiting seasons, we are full of imperfections—like rocks and debris in the clay. To prepare the clay to be molded, a potter will sift the clay to remove impurities, leaving the clay smooth, even, and easier to shape.

God wants to do the same thing in our lives. He wants to remove the things that hinder His work so we will be clean, soft, and ready to be molded into His desired form. Through these waiting seasons He carefully prepares us to become all He has called us to be and to be ready for the blessings He has for us.

The Power of Remaining in God's Will

God is so gracious that even if we get off at the wrong stop, He'll still be there to guide us back. He doesn't abandon us when we take a wrong turn. But the quicker we return to His will, the sooner we can get back on track toward the purpose He has for us.

Psalm 46:10 says, "Be still, and know that I am God." God is not delayed. He did not forget about you. He is always on time. Our responsibility is to remain in His will, trust His process, and know He will never leave us.

My vision of the train was a wake-up call, reminding me that impatience and frustration often come from a lack of trust. The conductor—God—knows exactly where He's taking us. Our job is not to rush the journey or take control but to trust that He is leading us toward the right destination at the right time.

> ## The journey isn't just about the destination—it's about the transformation that happens in us along the way.

If you're in a waiting season today, I encourage you to stay on the train. Trust the conductor. Don't get off prematurely just because the journey feels long or uncertain. You are exactly where you need to be, and if you can remain still, you will see God's perfect plan unfold. Friend, you will go forward. You will break out of the waiting. You will see the promises.

Believe it!

Is your life stormproof?

What are some areas of your life where you might need to focus on seeking God first rather than prioritizing your own desires or plans? What role does patience play in your relationship with God, and how can you cultivate more patience as you wait for His answers? How can you remind yourself that God is always on time, even when you don't understand why things are happening the way they are?

> *Father, thank You for reminding me that Your timing is perfect and You are at work, even when I can't see it. I confess that at times I feel frustrated, impatient, and tempted to take matters into my own hands. But I choose to trust that You know exactly what I need and*

when I need it. Help me be patient and wait with hope, even when the journey feels long. Give me the strength to stay faithful and remain focused on You, knowing that You are refining me and preparing me for what's ahead. I trust that You are with me, and I will wait on You, knowing that Your plans for me are good. In Jesus' name, amen.

Chapter 10

UNSHAKABLE FAITH

THE CLOSER YOU get to breakthrough, the harder it can be to keep believing. In this chapter I want to encourage you and stir your faith to keep pressing forward even when you're feeling tired, discouraged, or tempted to give up.

During a long drive to a tent revival in Kentucky, God spoke something profound to me. The journey was an hour and a half, and to be honest, I was exhausted. I didn't feel like driving, let alone ministering. As the miles stretched on, I started to feel weighed down—discouraged and critical of myself.

Somewhere along the drive I realized I had been following an ambulance the entire way. At first I didn't think much of it; I was just focused on getting to my destination. But then something remarkable happened. God began to speak to me through that ambulance in front of me.

An ambulance is essentially a mobile hospital rushing to those who are sick and in need. In that moment I felt God remind me of the church's calling. We are the hands and feet of Jesus, called to reach out to the broken and hurting. Just as an ambulance responds to emergencies, we are called to respond to the needs around us.

Think about it: The church isn't just a building—it's us. Each one of us is a vessel for God's love and healing. We are meant to be a refuge for the weary, a source of comfort for the grieving, and a light for those in darkness. God was encouraging me, reminding me that every act of kindness, every visit to the sick, and every word of hope we share makes us an ambulance for the soul. What a powerful revelation!

As I drove, I felt a fresh wave of energy wash over me. The weariness faded as I understood my assignment more clearly. God was showing me that my tiredness was a small price to pay for the privilege of sharing His love with others. Through this experience I discovered what it means to have unshakable faith.

The Faith to Keep Moving

An ambulance doesn't quit halfway to the hospital. It keeps going, no matter how rough the road may be. Unshakable faith works the same way—it pushes through difficulties, trusting that God is with us even when it feels like He's not.

> The church isn't just a building. Each one of us is a vessel for God's love and healing.

In 2 Kings 13 we see a story about perseverance and faith. The prophet Elisha told King Joash to take a bow and arrows and shoot an arrow out the window. As Joash did this, Elisha declared, "This is the Lord's arrow of victory, the victory over Aram!" (v. 17, paraphrased). Then Elisha told Joash to take the remaining arrows and strike the ground. Joash struck the ground three times and stopped.

Elisha was upset and essentially said, "You should have struck five or six times! Then you would have completely defeated Aram. But now, you'll only defeat them three times."

Each strike was an act of faith and perseverance. It symbolized believing for complete victory, even when the results weren't immediately visible. This story powerfully illustrates the importance of unshakable faith and persistence. We can't give up just because we don't see anything happening.

Keep striking the ground until you see the breakthrough! The king stopped too soon, and as a result he didn't achieve complete victory. The message is simple: You have to keep striking! Don't stop after just a few tries. Keep going, even when it's hard, because your breakthrough is coming.

Unshakable faith is about perseverance. When I was feeling down on that drive, God reminded me to keep pushing forward. Unshakable faith doesn't give up—it causes you to stay faithful even when you're tired or frustrated. Just like that ambulance stayed on course, we must keep moving toward the promises God has for us. You might feel like giving up, but you're closer than you think to the breakthrough you've been waiting for.

You don't stop after a few arrows. You don't stop after a few prayers. You keep striking the ground until you see the victory God has promised—until you see salvation in your family, restoration in your marriage, or complete freedom from addiction!

We can't quit when the storms come. We have to push through.

When Elisha told the king to strike the ground, it wasn't just a symbolic act for victory over Aram. There's a powerful lesson here about faith. Just as the king struck the ground repeatedly to ensure victory, every time you pray, every time you persevere even when you don't see results, you're striking the ground in faith.

It might feel like you're not getting anywhere, but remember this: Every strike is moving you closer to your breakthrough. When you feel like you can't go on, that's when you need to strike even harder. The victory is coming. You just have to continue pressing!

THE POWER OF PERSISTENT FAITH

In 2019 I received a prophetic word that God was going to give me a studio. At the time I didn't fully understand what that meant, nor did I desire it. It just seemed like a cool idea, but it wasn't something I was actively pursuing. But a few months later, supernatural events began to unfold.

One day a friend called to connect me with someone. When he

merged the call, I found myself speaking to a well-known man of God I had only heard of but never met. He told me he was in an airport about to board a flight and that God had given him specific instructions to help me with media and television. I was blown away. Just months earlier I had received that prophetic word about a studio, and now this man of God—who didn't even know me personally—was confirming it.

A month later, while I was at a conference in Atlanta, another man approached me out of nowhere and said, "God says, 'I'm placing this studio and cameras in your hands,'" and then walked off. By then I was freaking out. I had now received three separate words from different people about this studio.

But it didn't stop there. A few months later I was in Kentucky at another conference when yet another man whom I'd never met walked up to me and said he wanted to share something the Lord had shown him concerning me. He said, "I see God establishing you with your own media headquarters." By this point I was both confused and convinced that God was up to something big. It was clear God was about to open the door for a studio, but I still had no idea how His promise would come to pass.

Not long after that, the door opened. God provided a beautiful space with multiple offices, a kitchen, a lobby, and a large room that could serve as the studio itself. But the studio wasn't complete. We needed cameras, equipment, and new flooring.

So every day, I drove to the building, which was just ten minutes from my home, and prayed. I laid hands on the property, declaring in faith that this studio would be fully equipped. And slowly but surely, things began to fall into place.

The journey wasn't easy. After moving in, we faced a major challenge: The cost of the studio set, cameras, and equipment was nearly $40,000—an amount I didn't have. On top of that, we needed to renovate the space, install new flooring, and paint. It all seemed impossible.

But here's the thing: We didn't stop. My cousin Justin and I walked the halls, praying with unshakable faith and declaring that God would provide. We kept striking the ground, refusing to give up. We didn't have the money, but we knew God had promised this studio, so we kept acting in faith.

I remember ordering boxes of tiles for the flooring even though we didn't have the money yet. Then, out of nowhere, someone messaged me, saying they felt led to sow into the studio. They gave the exact amount needed to cover the flooring. This wasn't just a one-time thing, either. Over and over God provided exactly what we needed right when we needed it.

Keep striking the ground until you see the breakthrough!

Then came the big bill: $40,000 for the set. I was anxious about it, but I kept striking the ground in faith, believing God would come through. We raised most of it but still needed about $13,000. The final invoice was due, and I was down to the last few days. While on a ministry trip to Southern California, I received a call from the same well-known man of God who had contacted me at the beginning of this journey. He said he felt led to pay off the remaining balance for the set.

And just like that, God provided everything we needed—cameras, equipment, and the set—all paid in full. It was an overwhelming moment of gratitude and a powerful reminder of the power of persistent faith. When you keep striking the ground, when you keep believing even when it seems impossible, God will show up.

This studio didn't come to pass because of my own efforts. It happened because I kept pressing forward in faith. Even when I didn't have the resources, I kept taking steps of faith, declaring that God would provide—and He did, every single time. This experience deepened my faith, showing me that God answers when we keep striking the ground, keep believing, and keep trusting Him to orchestrate everything He promised.

I've learned that unshakable faith doesn't develop overnight. It's forged in moments when you're facing the impossible or going through storms that feel like they'll never end, and you choose to trust God anyway.

The thing that will sustain you through those times is understanding that God's perspective is way bigger than yours. We often view our challenges through the lens of the present. We see the financial struggles, broken relationships, sickness, or hurt and think, "This is it. This is the end of the story." We get overwhelmed by what's in front of us and feel like we're striking the ground but not breaking through. But God wants to remind you today that He sees the bigger picture.

Every time you strike the ground, every time you pray and persevere, you're aligning yourself with His plan. Even when you don't see the breakthrough yet, know that God is moving behind the scenes. He sees farther than you can right now. Trust that His promises are true and He is faithful to complete what He started.

Keep Going, Keep Believing

If you're feeling tired, frustrated, or ready to give up, let me remind you of the ambulance. It doesn't stop until it reaches its destination, and neither should you. Keep striking the ground. Keep believing, even when things don't seem to be going your way. Unshakable faith keeps moving forward, no matter how long the journey takes.

God is with you, and His promises are true. So whatever you're facing right now, don't give up. Keep going. Keep striking the ground in faith, trusting that breakthrough is closer than you think.

But as you persevere, I want to challenge you to look for the "ambulances" in your life—the people around you who are hurting and in need. Maybe it's a friend going through a tough time, a neighbor feeling lonely, or a coworker overwhelmed by life. Be that traveling hospital for them.

As the church, we are called to be the hands and feet of Jesus, a hospital for the broken. Let's respond to that call with compassion and purpose, just like an ambulance on a mission. Let's bring hope and healing wherever we go, sharing the love of Christ with a world in need.

Is your life stormproof?

Take a moment to think about your own life and the challenges you're facing right now. Do you feel like giving up? Where in your life do you need to press on and keep striking the ground in faith, even when the results aren't immediate? What small steps can you take today to keep moving forward with unshakable faith?

> *Lord, thank You for the reminder that unshakable faith is built through perseverance. I confess that sometimes I feel tired, frustrated, and ready to give up. But today I choose to keep striking the ground in faith. I trust You to provide, to lead me, and to fulfill the promises You've made over my life. Help me stay faithful even when I can't see the breakthrough yet. Show me how I can be a source of hope and healing to those around me, just like an ambulance rushing to those in need. In Jesus' name, amen.*

CHAPTER 11

LIVING WITH ETERNITY IN MIND

W E LIVE IN a world where everyone is always in a rush. We want immediate gratification and instant results. But when we look at how Jesus lived and what He taught, we see a different perspective—one that focuses on eternity. Living with eternity in mind changes everything. Our best life isn't here; it's in what's to come.

The truth is, everyone wants to go to heaven, but not everyone wants to live with a heavenly mindset while still on earth. I once read that our life down here compared to eternity is like a single drop in an ocean. How true is that?

James 4:14 reminds us, "Whereas you do not know what will happen tomorrow. For what is your life? It is even a vapor that appears for a little time and then vanishes away" (NKJV).

If our time here is short and eternity is forever, doesn't it make sense to focus on what truly matters? It's not about the possessions we collect or the achievements we chase. None of that goes with us when we step into eternity. You've probably heard the saying, "You'll never see a U-Haul behind a hearse." It's an old line, but it's so true. No matter how much stuff we accumulate in this life, none of it comes with us when we die.

We can't take our money, possessions, or status into eternity. Heaven and hell don't have banks, parking spots, or garages for us to store our stuff. When we leave this world, everything we obsess over here will stay behind.

I remember when I got a brand-new car. I was so excited—it felt perfect. But within the first week, things started going wrong. The seat belt button got chipped, then the charging port stopped working properly. Later, I walked out of a restaurant and noticed a deep scratch on my car, like someone had keyed it. Then, to top it off, a garage door accidentally came down on it while I was out of town.

Everyone wants to go to heaven, but not everyone wants to live with a heavenly mindset while still on earth.

I'm picky about details and love keeping things looking brand-new, so this was frustrating. But God used those moments to speak to me. He showed me how easily I had made that car an idol, putting my focus and energy on something that would ultimately fade away. He reminded me that I wouldn't be taking that car with me into eternity. God used those little mishaps to shift my perspective and remind me to value what truly matters—the things that are eternal, not the stuff we hold so tightly to in this life.

Jesus said it best in Matthew 6:19–20: "Do not store up for yourselves treasures on earth, where moths and vermin destroy, and where thieves break in and steal. But store up for yourselves treasures in heaven, where moths and vermin do not destroy, and where thieves do not break in and steal." And in Matthew 16:26 He asks, "For what profit is it to a man if he gains the whole world, and loses his own soul?" (NKJV).

We see so many people chasing after what the world offers, but let's get this straight: Following Jesus comes with a price, but not following Him costs even more. All the stuff we accumulate here on earth—money, fame, pleasure—is temporary. No matter how hard we try to hold on to it, it's all going to pass away.

First John 2:17 reminds us, "The world is passing away, and also its lusts; but the one who does the will of God lives forever" (NASB). Why trade that eternal reward for temporary things that won't last?

It's not wrong to enjoy nice things, but there's a huge difference between owning things and letting them own you. The truth is, money, cars, and houses won't matter when you stand before God. They can't change your eternal destination, no matter how much you have.

Take a moment to think about this: Whatever isn't eternal is worthless in eternity. Temporary things will fade away, but what's eternal can't be touched. Heavenly treasures are forever. Moths, rust, and thieves can't touch what is stored up for us in heaven. Your eternal reward is secure in God's hands, and eternity is what you should set your heart on.

How we view eternity affects how we live today. When we focus on what's eternal, it changes how we use our time, money, and energy. As 2 Corinthians 4:18 says, "while we do not look at the things which are seen, but at the things which are not seen. For the things which are seen are temporary, but the things which are not seen are eternal" (NKJV).

The choice is clear: Will you live for what's temporary or for what's eternal?

So often we act like the things we can see and touch are permanent. We cling to them, thinking they'll fulfill us. And for a moment they might—but it never lasts. Soon enough the satisfaction fades and we're back to chasing something else. It's a never-ending cycle.

Actor Jim Carrey, who has experienced fame, fortune, and success, once said, "I think everybody should get rich and famous and do everything they ever dreamed of so they can see that that's not the answer."[1]

You can chase all the pleasures and material things this world has to offer and still feel empty because they can't fill the longings of your heart. No matter how much stuff you have, no matter how many things you gain in this world, they will never satisfy the deep craving in your soul. Only the presence and love of God can do that.

So ask yourself: Are there things in your life that have become idols? Have you been trusting in people or possessions more than God? It's time to shift your focus. Start living with eternity in mind. Begin storing treasures in heaven, because this world is passing away.

Will you live for what's temporary or for what's eternal?

Are you living with the goal of reaching heaven, or are you coasting through life without considering your eternal destiny? One day we will all stand before God and give an account of how we lived. Let's make sure we're living for what truly matters.

Is your life stormproof?

Take a moment to reflect on your relationship with God. Is there anything in your life that you've made more important than Him? Are you holding on to things that God has called you to let go of? Are there areas where you've been focused on the temporary instead of the eternal? What steps can you take today to shift your focus and begin living with eternity in mind?

> *Father, thank You for reminding me that this life is short but eternity is forever. I confess that I've often gotten caught up in the temporary things of this world, chasing what pleases my flesh. Help me shift my focus and start living with eternity in mind. Show me the areas in my life where I need to let go and trust You more. I want to store up treasures in heaven, not on earth. I pray for the wisdom and strength to live with my eyes fixed on You and Your eternal purpose. In Jesus' name, amen.*

PART II

STORMPROOF
STUDY GUIDE

HOW TO USE THIS STUDY GUIDE

WELCOME TO THIS eleven-week study guide, a resource designed to help you deepen your faith, reflect on your spiritual journey, and strengthen your relationship with God. Each week builds on the truths we've been exploring, offering practical applications, reflection questions, and group discussion prompts to guide you through the study. Whether you're engaging with this guide on your own or in a small group setting, it's designed to challenge and inspire you to grow in your walk with Christ.

Here's how to get the most out of this study guide:

1. **Read the chapter content.** Begin each week by reading the corresponding chapter. The study guide includes key themes, Scripture references, and personal reflections to help you internalize the material.

2. **Take time to reflect.** Each week, you will find reflection questions meant to help you evaluate your experiences and spiritual journey. Use this time to get still, allowing the Holy Spirit to speak to your heart as you write your thoughts in a journal or notebook.

3. **Engage in group discussion.** If you're using this guide in a small group setting, the discussion questions are designed to spark meaningful conversations. Share your insights, learn from others, and grow together in faith.

4. **Apply the lessons.** Every chapter offers an action plan to help you put your faith into practice. Use

the weekly steps as a guide to living out what you've
learned in real, tangible ways.

5. **Memorize Scripture.** Each week concludes with a
verse for you to meditate on and memorize so you
can hide God's Word in your heart and carry His
truth with you throughout your day.

My prayer is that you'll use this study to let God's Word penetrate your heart and transform your life. I believe these truths will
help you build a firm foundation of faith and cultivate an unshakable trust in God.

Finally, while this study guide is ideal for small group settings,
you can use it for personal study. If you're diving into it individually,
consider setting aside dedicated time each week to work through
the material. For small groups, commit to meeting regularly to discuss insights and encourage one another in faith.

WEEK 1

THE FOUNDATION OF FAITH

I N THE GOSPEL of Matthew, Jesus shares a powerful parable about two builders: one who builds his house on rock and the other on sand. When storms come, the house on the rock stands firm while the house on the sand falls with a great crash (Matt. 7:24–27).

This parable reminds us of how crucial our foundation is in life. Just as a house that is built on a weak foundation can't withstand storms, our faith needs to be built on a solid foundation to endure every trial.

In this chapter I talk about what it means to build your life on the rock of Jesus Christ and how having a strong spiritual foundation is key to standing firm in the storms of life.

KEY THEMES

- **The importance of a strong foundation:** Jesus emphasizes that when storms come, the foundation we build on will determine whether we stand firm or fall apart. A foundation built on Christ and His Word provides the stability needed for every storm.

- **Hearing and doing the Word:** It's not enough to just hear the Word of God; we must put it into practice. James 1:22 warns against being "hearers only" and encourages us to be "doers" of the Word (MEV).

- **Temporary vs. eternal foundations:** The world offers temporary foundations (money, fame, possessions), but these things are unreliable.

- **Character development through trials:** God uses the storms of life to reveal our true character and shape us into the people He's called us to be. True faith is revealed in the midst of hardship.

- **The cost of building on rock:** Building on a solid foundation takes time, effort, and sacrifice. It requires intentionally abiding in Christ, being a student of the Scriptures, and applying the Word to our daily lives.

Personal Reflection

1. Have you ever experienced a "storm" or difficult trial? How did you respond?

2. When confronted with challenging situations, is your faith firm and unshaken, or do you feel like you're being tossed around?

3. What aspects of your life might be acting as a "sand" foundation, such as money, influence, career, or temporary pleasures?

4. Are you just hearing the Word of God, or are you actively living it out in your daily life?

Group Discussion

1. In the parable of the builders, what do you think Jesus is trying to teach us about the importance of obeying His Word?

2. What are some practical ways we can ensure we're building our lives on a solid foundation of faith rather than on the shifting sands of the world?

APPLICATION

- **Build on the Rock.** Jesus is the Rock, and building your life on Him means making Him the foundation of everything you do. This includes your decisions, relationships, finances, and even your emotions. Ask yourself, Is Jesus truly at the center of my life? Or have I been building on temporary things?

- **Actively apply the Word of God.** It's important to not just hear the Word of God but to live it out. This can be challenging in a world that encourages us to live based on worldly values. Begin by taking one specific teaching from Jesus (such as loving your neighbor or forgiving others) and making it a point to live it out this week.

- **Examine your foundation.** Take time this week to reflect on your life. What is your foundation built on? Are there areas where you've been building on sand? Ask God to reveal any weak spots and to help you strengthen your foundation in Him.

- **Surround yourself with support.** As the wise builder dug deep to build on solid rock, we must surround ourselves with godly influences. Find people who will encourage you in your faith and hold you accountable to live according to God's Word.

ACTION PLAN FOR THE WEEK

- **Practice daily devotions.** Set aside time each day to read and meditate on Scripture. Focus on passages that talk about building your life on Christ, such as Matthew 7:24–27, Colossians 2:6–7, and James 1:22.

- **Practice obedience.** Look for one area of your life where you can put God's Word into practice. Maybe it's forgiving someone, being more generous, or spending more time in prayer.

- **Examine your heart.** Reflect daily on your spiritual condition. Are there any "little foxes" (small sins or distractions) that are damaging your spiritual foundation? Take steps to address them.

- **Join a community.** If you're not already part of a small group or fellowship, make an effort to connect with others who will encourage you in your walk with God. Share your struggles and strengths with them.

MEMORY VERSE

Therefore everyone who hears these words of mine and puts them into practice is like a wise man who built his house on the rock. The rain came down, the streams rose, and the winds blew and beat against that house; yet it did not fall, because it had its foundation on the rock.

—MATTHEW 7:24–25

WEEK 2

THE ANCHOR OF YOUR FAITH

IT'S OFTEN SAID that we're either going through a storm, about to face one, or just coming out of one. In every storm, our faith is tested. The real question is, Where is our faith anchored? Just as a ship needs an anchor in order to stay secure during a storm, we need our faith anchored in God. Without this anchor, our faith can be tossed around by life's winds, leaving us vulnerable. This chapter emphasizes the importance of having our faith anchored in Christ and explains how we can weather every storm through Him.

KEY THEMES

- **Faith needs an anchor:** Without something to hold on to, faith can lead to spiritual instability. Having the right anchor is essential if we want to stand firm during life's storms. Jesus is our anchor.

- **Two ways of enduring tests:** The Lord showed me that there are two ways we go through tests of faith—without an anchor, and with Christ as our anchor. When we go through tests without faith that is anchored in Christ, life's storms can leave us feeling lost and overwhelmed. But when our faith is anchored in Jesus, we have the strength and peace to face any trial, knowing He is unchanging and faithful.

- **Lukewarm faith:** It's not enough to just acknowledge God occasionally. True discipleship requires a deep, daily commitment to follow Jesus, not just going through the motions.

- **The purpose of trials:** Trials are meant to strengthen our faith and draw us closer to Christ. Whether we go through them unanchored or anchored, tests are used by God to shape us into the image of His Son.

PERSONAL REFLECTION

1. Reflect on your current season. Are you currently in a storm, coming out of one, or about to face one? How do you feel?

2. Have you ever felt that your faith was drifting or uncertain during tough times? What served as your anchor during that season—relationships, material possessions, or routines? How did that help or fail you?

3. I experienced a profound transformation after having an encounter with Jesus at nineteen years old. Think about your own experiences with Jesus. Was there a time when you realized you weren't going to just believe in God but fully surrender to Him? What changed when your faith became more personal?

GROUP DISCUSSION

1. Share a time when you felt overwhelmed by life's storms. How did you handle it?

2. Why do you think God allows us to go through tests in life? How do these tests shape our character and faith?

3. I talk about two ways we endure tests of faith: without an anchor and with Christ as our anchor. Share examples of when you went through tests in either of these ways in your own life. How did your faith change as a result?

4. What might having "faith without an anchor" look like in a person's life? How would it affect their emotional and/or spiritual stability?

5. How can we move from being "lukewarm" to having a more committed and passionate faith in Christ?

6. What are some practical ways we can ensure that our faith remains anchored in Christ, especially during difficult times?

APPLICATION

- **Anchor your faith in Christ.** Make sure your faith is anchored in Jesus, not just in religious routines or superficial beliefs. Seek a deeper relationship with Him. Spend time in prayer, study the Bible, and actively follow His teachings.

- **Embrace the storms.** Instead of avoiding or complaining about the storms, learn to embrace them as opportunities for growth. Trust that God is using them to strengthen your faith and deepen your relationship with Him.

- **Be committed.** Reflect on your level of commitment to Jesus. Are you just going through the motions, or are you all in, surrendering every part of your life to

Him? Take steps to grow in your faith and take up your cross daily.

- **Build your foundation.** Strengthen your spiritual foundation. Read the Bible daily.

Action Plan for the Week

- **Reflect daily.** Each day, spend five to ten minutes reflecting on the state of your faith. Are you anchored in Christ, or are you relying on temporary things to get by? Write your thoughts in a journal.

- **Pray daily.** Take time each day this week to pray for greater intimacy with Jesus.

- **Commit to daily devotions.** Start a habit of making appointments with God.

- **Look for opportunities to serve.** This week, look for ways to serve others, whether through acts of kindness, helping a neighbor, encouraging a friend, or something else the Lord leads you to do.

- **Evaluate your commitments.** Are you fully committed to following Jesus, or are you casual with Him in certain areas of your life? Identify one area where you can grow in your relationship with Jesus.

Memory Verse

You will keep in perfect peace those whose minds are steadfast, because they trust in you.

—Isaiah 26:3

THE REFINING

I N THIS CHAPTER we explore how trials and hardships are like the refining fire that purifies gold. Just as gold is heated in fire to remove impurities, we are often placed in "fiery" trials that reveal hidden things in our hearts. The heat in these seasons exposes fears, pride, bitterness, and other impurities, allowing God to purify us and make us more like Christ.

One analogy that illustrates this concept is the sauna. In a sauna, the intense heat opens your pores, causing sweat to bring impurities to the surface. Spiritually, when we are in the Refiner's fire, the heat of those trials opens the "pores" of our hearts and causes the impurities to rise to the surface—things we may not have been aware of, such as fear or unforgiveness. This process is not comfortable, but it is necessary for growth.

KEY THEMES

- **Refining through trials:** Trials are like fire, revealing the impurities in our hearts. The heat of these trials forces us to confront areas of our lives that need to be purified, just like heat in a sauna causes impurities to rise to the surface.

- **God's purpose in the crushing:** In much the same way gold must be heated to be purified, God uses trials to purify our faith and remove what doesn't belong. This process is not easy, but it is necessary for spiritual growth.

- **Emptying ourselves for God's filling:** Just like a vessel must be emptied to be filled, we need to empty ourselves of pride, unforgiveness, and distractions so that God can fill us with His presence.

- **The role of discipleship:** The Israelites needed to let go of their Egyptian mindset, and many of us need to let go of old habits and ways of thinking. What are some old mindsets or behaviors you need to surrender to God?

- **Ministering through brokenness:** As the crushing of olives produces oil, our brokenness allows God to create something beautiful and useful for His kingdom. Our trials can equip us to comfort others in their struggles.

PERSONAL REFLECTION

1. Think about a time when you faced a personal struggle or trial. How did it feel? What came to the surface in your heart during that time? Were there emotions, fears, or attitudes you didn't realize were there before? Reflect on how those moments of heat or pressure might have been God's way of refining your heart and faith.

2. What impurities in your heart have trials revealed?

3. How do you respond when life gets uncomfortable or "heated"?

4. In what areas are you resisting God's refining fire?

GROUP DISCUSSION

1. The heat in a sauna opens your pores and causes impurities to rise to the surface. How is this similar to the trials we face in life? What kind of impurities might God be bringing to the surface in your life through trials?

2. In 1 Peter 1:6–7, Peter compares trials to the process of refining gold in fire. How does the analogy of the heat and pressure of trials bring clarity to how we grow spiritually?

3. The heat of the sauna is not meant to harm the body but to cleanse it. Similarly, the trials we face are not meant to destroy us but to purify us. How can we trust that God's purpose in our trials is for our good, even when we feel uncomfortable?

4. In the same way a clogged sink prevents water from flowing freely, sometimes our hearts are blocked by sin, fear, or pride. How can we identify the "clogs" in our lives and allow God to remove them so His Spirit can flow freely?

APPLICATION

- **Embrace the heat.** Just as stepping into a sauna might be uncomfortable at first, embrace the discomfort of trials, knowing God is using them to refine and purify you. Ask God to help you see His purpose in these trials and trust Him in the process.

- **Identify the impurities.** Reflect on areas of your heart where fear, pride, or unforgiveness might be hiding.

Ask God to bring these impurities to the surface so He can remove them and make you more like Christ.

- **Encourage yourself in the Lord.** Reflect on how God has used trials in your life to refine and purify you. Pray that you will be willing to embrace the heat and allow God to change you through it.

Action Plan for the Week

- **Reflect daily.** Take time each day to reflect on any trials or struggles you're facing. Ask God to reveal what He might be purifying in your heart during these times.

- **Surrender impurities.** Identify any "impurities"—bitterness, fear, pride, and so on—that are rising to the surface in your life. Surrender these to God and ask Him to cleanse you.

- **Help someone else.** If you know someone who is going through a difficult season, encourage them. Remind them that God uses the heat to refine us, and share your own experiences of how God has used trials in your life.

- **Seek God's presence.** Spend extra time in prayer this week, asking God to fill you with more of His Spirit. Let go of distractions and allow Him to refine you, knowing He is shaping you for His purposes.

Memory Verse

These have come so that the proven genuineness of your faith—of greater worth than gold, which perishes even though refined by fire—may result in praise, glory and honor when Jesus Christ is revealed.

—1 Peter 1:7

THE POWER OF SONSHIP

I N THIS CHAPTER we dive into the powerful concept of sonship—understanding our identity as sons and daughters of the Most High God. Through the story of Zechariah 3, the experiences of the pastor from South Texas, and personal reflections, we see how embracing our sonship in Christ changes everything. This study guide will help us reflect on the key themes, apply these lessons to our lives, and strengthen our understanding of the privileges and responsibilities of being part of God's family.

KEY THEMES

- **The gift of sonship:** God's love is not something we earn but a gift of grace. Like Joshua in Zechariah 3, we stand before God in our "filthy clothes" (our sin), but He chooses to forgive and cleanse us. When we accept Christ, God gives us a new identity, and we are no longer defined by sin but by grace.

- **God chooses us:** God thought about us long before we ever thought about Him. John 15:16 and Ephesians 2:8–9 remind us that salvation and sonship are God's decisions. They are not based on our works.

- **Rejection vs. acceptance:** Rejection can deeply affect our self-worth, but when we understand we are accepted by God, rejection loses its power. Just as Jesus offered the woman at the well a new identity, He offers us the same—grace, forgiveness, and love.

- **Living out our sonship:** Our new identity changes the way we live, interact with others, and carry the presence of God. Romans 8:38–39 reassures us that nothing can separate us from the love of God. As sons and daughters of God, we are carriers of His favor and hope, transforming the atmosphere around us.

Personal Reflection

1. Reflect on your identity. How do you currently see yourself? Are you living in the fullness of your identity as a child of God, or are there areas where you struggle with feelings of rejection or inadequacy?

2. How has understanding your sonship in Christ changed the way you view your relationship with God?

3. The pastor's testimony of coming to realize that he couldn't earn God's love resonated deeply with me. Have you ever struggled with trying to earn God's favor or love? How does it feel to know that God's love is unconditional and based on His grace alone?

4. Reflect on times when you've faced rejection. How did it affect your self-worth and behavior? How does knowing that God fully accepts you change your perspective on rejection?

Group Discussion

1. Discuss the vision of Joshua in Zechariah 3. How does God's act of removing Joshua's filthy clothes and

giving him new garments illustrate His grace and the gift of sonship?

2. In what ways does understanding that God chose us (rather than us choosing Him) impact how we live out our faith? How does this knowledge affect your confidence in your relationship with God?

3. Share a time when you felt rejected and how that affected you. How can understanding your identity in Christ help you overcome feelings of rejection in the future?

4. How does knowing that you are a son or daughter of God change the way you interact with the world? Have you noticed shifts in your life as you grow in your understanding of this identity?

APPLICATION

- **Embrace your new identity.** Start each day by reminding yourself of your new identity in Christ. You are not defined by your mistakes or failures but by God's love and grace. You are a child of the Most High God.

- **Let go of rejection.** If feelings of rejection or insecurity are holding you back, take time this week to reflect on God's acceptance of you. Whenever feelings of rejection arise, combat them with the truth that you are loved and accepted by God.

- **Walk in the favor of God.** Recognize that as a child of God you carry His presence wherever you go. This week, intentionally live out your identity by bringing hope, peace, and change to the environments around you. When you walk into a room, know that the atmosphere shifts because you carry the presence of God.

Action Plan for the Week

- **Practice daily affirmations.** Spend five minutes each morning declaring your identity in Christ. Tell yourself, "I am a child of God. I am forgiven, accepted, and loved. God has chosen me."

- **Reject rejection.** This week, when you feel rejected by people, circumstances, or even yourself, remind yourself of your worth in Christ.

  Say aloud, "I am accepted by God, and His love is enough for me."

- **Impact the atmosphere.** Take note of your environment this week at work, school, home, or social gatherings. How can you bring God's peace and hope into these spaces? Be intentional about bringing joy and encouragement to others.

Memory Verse

For I am convinced that neither death nor life, neither angels nor demons, neither the present nor the future, nor any powers, neither height nor depth, nor anything else in all creation, will be able to separate us from the love of God that is in Christ Jesus our Lord.

—Romans 8:38–39

WEEK 5

UNCOMPROMISING FAITH

I N CHAPTER 5 we discuss the powerful example of Shadrach, Meshach, and Abednego and their unwavering faith in the face of the fiery furnace. This story from Daniel 3 not only teaches us about standing firm in our beliefs; it also challenges us to live with an uncompromising faith in a world that constantly pressures us to bow down to Baal. Just like these three young men, we are called to take a stand for God—even when the fire of life's challenges gets hotter.

Shadrach, Meshach, and Abednego didn't just face a literal fire; they were in the midst of a spiritual fire, a test of faith. Their names had been changed and their identities distorted, but their commitment to God was unwavering. Let's uncover the lessons we can apply to our own lives.

KEY THEMES

- **Uncompromising faith:** Like Shadrach, Meshach, and Abednego, who refused to bow down to the idol, we are called to stand firm in our faith. True faith does not bend or bow to the pressures of the world but stands on the promises of God, regardless of the cost.

- **The test of faith:** The fiery furnace symbolizes the tests and trials we face in life. As Shadrach, Meshach, and Abednego stood firm in their faith, we too are called to remain faithful amid trials. True faith is trusting God even when we don't know the outcome.

- **God's presence in the fire:** When Shadrach, Meshach, and Abednego were thrown into the furnace, God didn't deliver them from the fire—He walked with them through it. While we often pray to be saved from the fire, that is where their chains were burned off. God wants to reveal His presence in powerful ways.

- **Our identity in Christ:** The enemy will attempt to strip us of our identity, just as King Nebuchadnezzar changed the names of these men in an attempt to redefine who they were. We must remind ourselves daily that our true identity is found in Christ, not in the world.

- **The power of praise:** Praise is a weapon, and even in the midst of trials, we are called to worship God. In the same way Shadrach, Meshach, and Abednego refused to let their circumstances bind their praise, we must choose to worship God through all situations.

- **The danger of bowing to sin:** Too often, we see how close we can get to sin without actually falling in. But the closer we get to the line, the more we risk everything. Scripture doesn't tell us to manage temptation—it tells us to *flee* from it (2 Tim. 2:22).

- **The call to stand firm:** In a world full of compromise, God is calling us to stand firm in our faith. We must live out a faith that does not bend to the world's standards but remains true to God's Word.

PERSONAL REFLECTION

Reflect on your own life and faith. Have you ever been tempted to compromise your beliefs to fit in? What was the outcome? How did you feel afterward?

1. Think about a time when your faith was tested. What was the "fire" you walked through? How did you respond? Did you feel God's presence with you in that moment?

2. Like Nebuchadnezzar attempted with Shadrach, Meshach, and Abednego, the enemy often tries to change our identity. Are there areas in your life where you feel pressured to bow to the world's standards? How can you stand firm in your true identity as a child of God?

3. Think about a time when you found yourself walking dangerously close to the line of temptation. What drew you in, and what ultimately helped you resist— or caused you to stumble? How did that experience impact your relationship with God? What steps can you take in the future to flee from temptation rather than flirt with it?

GROUP DISCUSSION

1. Why do you think Shadrach, Meshach, and Abednego refused to bow to the statue, even knowing it could cost them their lives?

2. What does it mean for us that God doesn't always deliver us from the fire but sometimes walks with us

through it? How can we find comfort in knowing that God is present in our trials?

3. How do we as believers face pressure to compromise our faith in today's world? How can we stand firm like Shadrach, Meshach, and Abednego did?

4. How did King Nebuchadnezzar try to strip Shadrach, Meshach, and Abednego of their identity? How does this apply to our modern lives, where the world is constantly challenging our identity?

5. Discuss how God honors those who stand firm in their faith. What promises has He given to those who remain uncompromising? Share any personal stories or testimonies of how God has shown His faithfulness in your life.

6. Why is praise and worship a powerful weapon when facing trials? Have you ever experienced a breakthrough during a difficult time through worship?

APPLICATION

- **Evaluate your stand.** Take a moment to reflect on areas where you may be compromising your faith. Have there been circumstances that have made you feel pressure to conform? Ask God to give you the strength to stand firm in those situations.

- **Worship in the fire.** This week, when facing struggles or spiritual warfare, intentionally use praise as your weapon. Worship can break through the toughest situations.

- **Check your identity.** Examine how you view your identity. Are you defining yourself by your circumstances, successes, or failures? Ask God to remind you of your true identity as His child, chosen and beloved.

- **Encourage one another.** Reflect on a time when you faced a spiritual fire or trial. How did you respond, and how did God's presence help you through it? Consider how you can stand firm in faith and continue praising God even when it's hard.

ACTION PLAN FOR THE WEEK

- **Stand firm in your faith.** This week, identify any area where you may be tempted to compromise. Take a stand for your faith even if it's uncomfortable. Let your decision be a testimony to those around you of your unwavering confidence in God.

- **Praise through the fire.** When faced with challenges this week, make an intentional effort to praise God through the struggle. Use worship as a tool to strengthen your faith and invite God's presence into your situation.

- **Affirm your identity in Christ.** Spend time in prayer, reminding yourself of who you are in Christ. Resist the pressure to fit in. Reaffirm your identity as a child of God, chosen, loved, and called for a purpose.

- **Be an encourager.** Encourage someone who may be struggling with compromising their faith. Share the story of Shadrach, Meshach, and Abednego with them, and remind them that God is with them in the fire.

MEMORY VERSE

When you walk through the fire, you will not be burned; the flames will not set you ablaze.

—ISAIAH 43:2

WEEK 6

COUNTERFEIT FAITH

IN TODAY'S WORLD, especially in the Western church, we face a troubling trend of complacency in our faith. It's easy to attend church, serve in ministries, and say the right things, but the heart of the matter is this: Is our faith genuine? Are we being transformed by the power of the gospel, or are we simply going through the motions?

In this chapter I talk about the difference between a counterfeit faith—a faith that looks good on the outside but lacks transformation—and a genuine faith that leads to a heart-level change. We look at Jesus' words, the example of the rich young ruler, and how we are called to be more than just churchgoers; we are to be transformed followers of Christ.

KEY THEMES

- **The danger of lukewarm Christianity:** Church attendance does not equate to a transformed life. We are called to reflect Christ in our thoughts, actions, and hearts.

- **Counterfeit faith vs. genuine faith:** A counterfeit faith is focused on outward appearances or seeking personal gain (like Simon in Acts 8), while genuine faith leads to heart transformation, obedience, and a deeper relationship with Jesus.

- **Transformation through surrender:** Genuine faith involves surrendering all areas of our lives to Jesus. It's not about asking what God can do for us but allowing Him to change us from the inside out.

- **The cross and discipleship:** Being a true disciple of Christ requires a willingness to lay down our lives for Him, not just to seek blessings. Jesus did not die to make us comfortable; He died to make us holy.

PERSONAL REFLECTION

1. What does the term *lukewarm Christianity* mean to you? Reflect on times when you may have been going through the motions in your faith—attending church and serving in ministry but not truly reflecting Christ in your daily life.

2. Is your faith leading to transformation? Take a moment to honestly evaluate your relationship with Jesus. Are you concerned with blessings and benefits, or are you committed to following Him with your whole heart, exchanging your will for His?

3. Think about the story of the rich young ruler in Matthew 19:16–22. Are there things in your life, like the rich young ruler's possessions, that have more control over you than your relationship with Christ? What is Jesus asking you to surrender today?

GROUP DISCUSSION

1. What are some characteristics of counterfeit faith? What are some signs of a genuine, transformed faith?

2. Discuss the difference between attending church and truly following Christ. How can we avoid falling into the trap of "attendance without transformation"?

3. In Acts 8, Simon's faith was counterfeit, while the Ethiopian eunuch's faith was genuine. What made their faith different?

4. How can we move from having a "form of godliness" to experiencing the true power of the gospel in our lives?

5. What does it mean to repent in the context of chapter 6? How do we know when we are truly living in a state of repentance and not just going through the motions?

Application

- **Evaluate your faith.** Ask yourself, Is my faith merely an external practice, or has it caused a deep, internal transformation? Do my everyday actions and attitudes reflect Christ's love and character?

- **Surrender and repent.** Identify any areas in your life where you are holding on to comfort, control, or worldly desires. Surrender these to Jesus and ask for His strength to make a change.

- **Seek true discipleship.** Commit to engaging in personal Bible study, prayer, and community with other believers. Discipleship is more than just church attendance; it's about growing in your relationship with Jesus and reflecting His character.

ACTION PLAN FOR THE WEEK

- **Make time for daily reflection.** Each day, set aside time to examine your heart. Ask the Holy Spirit to show you any areas of your life where you need transformation. Journal what God reveals to you.

- **Live out your faith.** This week, take intentional steps to live out your faith in tangible ways. Show love, patience, kindness, and humility to those around you. Reflect Christ's character in your actions, not just in your words.

- **Engage in discipleship.** Find a Bible study group or a mentor who can help you grow in your faith. Commit to reading a few chapters of the Bible each day and spend quality time in the presence of God.

- **Pray for boldness and transformation.** Ask God for the courage to embrace the cross and deny yourself. Pray for genuine, heart-level transformation, that your faith may reflect the power of the gospel.

MEMORY VERSE

Do not conform to the pattern of this world, but be transformed by the renewing of your mind. Then you will be able to test and approve what God's will is—his good, pleasing and perfect will.

—ROMANS 12:2

WEEK 7

FAITH IN ACTION

I N CHAPTER 7, I share a powerful personal experience of being lost in the desert and learning the importance of "following the Cloud." As the Israelites were guided through the wilderness by the presence of God in the form of a pillar of cloud by day and fire by night, we are called to follow God's presence in our lives.

This chapter challenges us to live out our faith by taking practical steps of obedience as well as trusting God's direction and responding to His promptings, even when it's inconvenient. The message is clear: True faith is not just about belief; it is about action. We must follow God's leading even when we can't see the whole picture or the path is difficult.

KEY THEMES

- **God's presence as our guide:** The Israelites were guided through the wilderness by a pillar of cloud by day and fire by night. This cloud was not just a symbol of God's presence; it directed their path (Exod. 13:21–22). Today, God's presence, through the Holy Spirit, continues to guide us in our faith walk. In the same way the Israelites moved when the cloud moved, we are called to follow God's leading in our lives.

- **The Cloud vs. the crowd:** The crowd represents the popular, easy, and often misleading path. Jesus warned that many will follow the broad road that leads to destruction (Matt. 7:13–14). The Cloud, on the other hand, symbolizes God's presence and the narrow road that leads to life. Following the Cloud often means going against the flow of culture and societal pressures. Today we are constantly being challenged to choose between following the crowd and following the Cloud, as the values of the world often conflict with the teachings of Jesus.

- **Faith requires action:** The Israelites had to follow the cloud in order to reach the Promised Land. We too must actively respond to God's call in our lives, even when it's difficult or uncomfortable, to fulfill His purpose. Faith in action involves trusting God's way and taking steps of obedience.

- **Following God when it's inconvenient:** Following the Cloud isn't always about blessings, and the path it leads us on won't always be easy. At times it calls us to step into uncomfortable situations, make sacrifices, or do things that don't immediately make sense—like forgiving when it's difficult or stepping out of our comfort zones to witness to someone. My experience in the desert has taught me that when we follow God even in inconvenient or challenging circumstances, we can trust that He is guiding us exactly where we need to be.

- **Divine appointments and obedience:** God often gives us divine appointments, when He wants to use us to bless others. Seizing these moments requires us to listen to the Holy Spirit's promptings, step out in faith, and move without hesitation. My story about giving money to the man in a yellow jacket at the gas station illustrates the power of obedience to the leading of the Holy Spirit even when it seems strange or inconvenient.

PERSONAL REFLECTION

1. Take a moment to reflect on your own walk with God. Are you truly following His path for you, or are you trying to walk your own way?

2. Have you ever felt lost or uncertain about where God is leading you? How did you respond?

3. Are there areas in your life where you're avoiding obedience because it's inconvenient or uncomfortable?

4. When you face challenges, do you trust that God's presence will guide you, or do you try to solve problems on your own? As you reflect, ask God to reveal any areas where you need to trust Him more fully and step out in faith. Open your heart to the Holy Spirit and ask for His guidance in taking action.

GROUP DISCUSSION

1. What does following the Cloud mean to you? How do you recognize when God is leading you in a particular direction?

2. Have you ever experienced a time when following God's way was inconvenient or uncomfortable? How did you respond?

3. In what areas of your life are you currently being challenged to step out in faith and follow God's direction, even when you don't see the whole picture?

4. I talk about the choice between following the crowd and following the Cloud. How can you resist the pressure of the crowd and stay focused on obeying God's will?

5. How do you differentiate between the crowd (the world's influence) and the Cloud (God's guidance)? What can help you stay on the narrow path that leads to life?

6. Have you ever had a divine appointment where God used you to impact someone else's life? What was it like, and how did you respond?

Application

- **Look for God's presence.** Start each day by asking God to guide you. Be intentional about seeking His direction in your life through prayer, His Word, and the Holy Spirit.

- **Step out in faith.** This week, identify one area where you feel God is calling you to take action. Whether it's reaching out to someone, stepping into a new opportunity, or making a difficult decision, take that first step of obedience.

- **Follow God's leading, even when it's hard.** Trust that God's presence will guide you even when the path ahead feels unclear or uncomfortable. Look for divine appointments—moments when God is calling you to take action—and don't hesitate to follow His prompting.

- **Resist the crowd.** Make a conscious effort to resist the influence of the crowd and the pressure of the culture. Spend time reflecting on what pleases God and choose to follow that, even if it means going against the norm.

ACTION PLAN FOR THE WEEK

- **Pray daily.** Commit to praying each morning, asking God to guide you and help you recognize His presence in your life.

- **Take a step of faith.** Identify a specific area where you need to follow God's leading. Take a step in that direction this week, even if it feels uncomfortable or uncertain.

- **Reflect on the Cloud and the crowd.** Throughout the week, think about the paths you're tempted to follow. Are you choosing the crowd (the easy path) or the Cloud (the path of obedience)? Make decisions based on God's guidance, not cultural pressure.

MEMORY VERSE

Your word is a lamp to my feet and a light to my path.
—PSALM 119:105, NKJV

WEEK 8

FUEL YOUR FAITH

HAPTER 8, "FUEL Your Faith," emphasizes the importance of strengthening our spiritual immunity through regular prayer and by nurturing our relationship with God. As our physical bodies need vitamins and nutrients to stay healthy, our spiritual lives require consistent attention, nourishment, and care. The idea is simple: We wouldn't wait until we're sick to take vitamins, and we shouldn't wait until we're spiritually weak or in crisis to pray. By maintaining a regular connection with God, we are better prepared to face the trials and temptations that come our way.

In this chapter I draw a powerful parallel between our physical health and our spiritual well-being. Just as we take intentional steps to keep our immune systems strong, we must also build spiritual immunity through prayer, studying the Word, and worshipping the Lord.

KEY THEMES

- **Strengthening your spiritual immunity:** In the same way our bodies need regular nourishment to stay healthy, our spirits need daily prayer and connection with God. Prayer is a spiritual "vitamin" that strengthens us and prepares us to face spiritual battles.

- **The importance of consistency:** Prayer is not just for times of crisis. Like vitamins we take regularly to maintain good health, prayer should be a regular practice to keep our spiritual lives strong.

- **Guarding our hearts and minds:** Galatians 6:8 reminds us that what we sow (focus on) will determine the fruit we reap. If we focus on the Spirit, we reap life; if we focus on the flesh, we reap destruction. Regular prayer and Bible reading are essential for cultivating a heart that seeks after God and grows spiritually.

- **Ascension and intimacy with God:** Psalm 24:4 tells us that to climb the mountain of the Lord, we must clean our hands (actions) and purify our hearts (intentions). This requires us to examine our lives and ensure that we heed the verse's instructions.

- **The rewards of a devoted prayer life:** As we spend time with God in prayer, we not only experience spiritual transformation but also receive the blessings and peace that come from being in His presence. Prayer draws us closer to God and strengthens our inner man.

PERSONAL REFLECTION

1. Take a moment to reflect on your prayer life. Are you nourishing your spirit regularly, or are you seeking God only when you're in trouble?

2. How do you usually respond to hardships? Do you pray immediately, or do you first try to handle things on your own?

3. When was the last time you spent quality, undistracted time in prayer?

4. How would your spiritual health change if you spent time each day strengthening your spirit with prayer and Scripture?

5. Consider how your spiritual health might improve if you made prayer a regular, daily priority, in the same way you make time for other important things in your life, like meals, work, or rest.

GROUP DISCUSSION

1. How does praying regularly help you stay spiritually strong? Can you think of a time when prayer helped you through a difficult situation?

2. What are some common distractions that make it hard to commit to regular prayer? How can we overcome them?

3. Just as we take vitamins to strengthen our immune systems, what "spiritual vitamins" do you rely on to strengthen your faith?

4. In what ways can we support one another in building stronger spiritual immune systems?

5. Chapter 8 compares spiritual health to tasks like washing our hands or fueling our cars. What other everyday activities have spiritual parallels?

6. How can small, daily habits build your faith in the same way small actions like brushing your teeth or eating well help you maintain your physical health?

APPLICATION

- **Prioritize prayer.** Reflecting on the analogy of vitamins, think of prayer as something that needs to be
  a daily practice, not just something we do in times
  of spiritual sickness. Set aside intentional time each
  day to pray, even if it's just for a few minutes, to
  strengthen your spiritual immunity.

- **Start small.** If you struggle with consistency, start
  with a simple habit—whether it's praying in the
  morning, reading a verse from the Bible, or taking
  a moment to turn down the noise and listen to God.
  The goal is to make these habits a part of your daily
  routine.

- **Examine your heart.** Chapter 8 challenges us to
  evaluate whether our lives are out of order. Consider
  areas in your life where you may be neglecting your
  relationship with God. Has anything become a "lesser
  lover" in your life, taking priority over your relationship with Jesus?

- **Encourage each other.** As a group, commit to
  praying for one another. Share prayer requests and
  pray together for spiritual strength and growth. We
  are stronger when we build one another up in faith.

ACTION PLAN FOR THE WEEK

- **Make time to pray daily.** Set a goal to spend at least
  thirty minutes in prayer each day. Use this time to
  express your gratitude, ask for the knowledge of His
  will, and listen for God's voice.

- **Get an accountability partner.** Connect with a friend or fellow believer each week to check in. Share updates on your prayer time and encourage each other to stay faithful in prayer.

- **Examine your spiritual life.** Take time this week to assess your spiritual life. Are there any idols or distractions in your heart that are taking priority over God? If so, repent and realign your focus.

MEMORY VERSE

Finally, be strong in the Lord and in his mighty power. Put on the full armor of God, so that you can take your stand against the devil's schemes.

—EPHESIANS 6:10–11

WEEK 9

TRUST THE PROCESS

IN THIS CHAPTER we talk about the importance of trusting God's timing and His process in our lives. Through personal reflections, the story of a vision on a train, and lessons from waiting on luggage, we learn how impatience can lead us off course and how God uses waiting seasons to refine us.

KEY THEMES

- **The struggle to wait:** Waiting is difficult, especially in a world that wants instant results. But God's timing is perfect, even when it feels slow. Trusting God means recognizing that His plans for us are always on time, even when we don't understand them.

- **Impatience and taking control:** Just like getting off a train prematurely or rushing to find a faster route, many of us try to take matters into our own hands when God's timing doesn't line up with our desires. But stepping out of His will can cause us to miss out on His perfect plan.

- **The power of remaining in God's will:** Even when the journey feels long or uncertain, staying in God's will is the key to experiencing His blessings. Impatience can delay our progress, but God's process prepares us for what's ahead.

- **God's timing and withholding:** Sometimes God withholds what we want not because He doesn't want to bless us but because He is preparing us. He refines our character and desires so we can receive His blessings at the right time, in the right way.

- **The transformation in the waiting:** Waiting isn't just about God's timing to reach the destination; it's about the transformation that happens in us as we wait. God uses the waiting season to purify us and mold us into the people He has called us to be.

PERSONAL REFLECTION

1. Are you currently in a waiting season? What have you been waiting on or praying for? How does waiting feel for you—frustrating, uncertain, or peaceful? Why?

2. Think of a time when you were impatient and tried to take control of your situation. What happened as a result? How did God redirect you back to His plan?

3. Have you ever had a situation where you saw the reason for the wait only after it passed? Reflect on how trusting God's process in the past has shaped your trust in His future plans for you.

4. Are there things you are praying for that you feel have been delayed? How do you feel about waiting for God's perfect timing in those areas? How might God be refining you in the process?

GROUP DISCUSSION

1. In the vision God gave me, I stepped off the train because of impatience. How does this reflect our

tendency to step out of God's will when we don't see immediate results? What are some common ways we take control when God is asking us to wait?

2. How can trusting God's timing lead to peace and growth? Share about a time when waiting on God's perfect timing led to a better outcome than rushing ahead.

3. How have you seen your character grow or change in the waiting season? What are some lessons God has taught you while you've been waiting for something to unfold?

4. When we desire something, how can we ensure our desires align with God's will? How does seeking God first, as Jesus instructs in Matthew 6:33, change our approach to waiting and praying?

APPLICATION

- **Trust the process.** Commit to trusting God's process even when it's hard. When you feel frustrated with waiting, take a moment to remind yourself that God's timing is always perfect. Trust that He is doing something in you as you wait.

- **Stay on track.** When you feel tempted to step off the path or take matters into your own hands, remind yourself of God's track record of faithfulness in the past. Stay focused on the journey and resist the urge to "reroute" because of impatience.

- **Reflect and let go.** Take time to reflect on areas where impatience has taken hold in your life. What desires or dreams have you rushed to achieve? Ask God to help you release the pressure of achieving those things on your own and trust Him to lead you to the right destination.

ACTION PLAN FOR THE WEEK

- **Practice patience.** Spend a few minutes each morning praying for patience and trust in God's timing. Declare out loud, "I trust God's process, and I am confident He is ordering my steps."

- **Reaffirm God's timing.** When you feel like rushing ahead or taking matters into your own hands, pause and think of God's perfect timing. Remind yourself, "God's timing is never late; it is always on time."

- **Embrace the waiting.** Choose one area in which you've been impatient, and commit to waiting with a sense of peace and trust. Each time you feel anxious about the outcome, pray and reaffirm your trust in God's process.

MEMORY VERSE

Wait for the LORD; be strong and take heart and wait for the LORD.

—PSALM 27:14

WEEK 10

UNSHAKABLE FAITH

N CHAPTER 10 the focus is on the power of unshakable faith—
faith that doesn't give up, even when we're discouraged or tired
or we feel like quitting. I share a personal story of how God
used a simple experience—a drive to a tent revival in Kentucky—to
give me a unique revelation about the church's mission. Unshakable faith is not about avoiding discouraging moments. It's about
pushing through them, trusting that God is with us, and continuing to move forward in obedience.

KEY THEMES

- **Faith and perseverance:** Unshakable faith is not
  about seeing immediate results; it's about continuing
  to press on despite fatigue, discouragement, or obstacles. It's about trusting that God will fulfill His
  promises.

- **The church is a hospital for the hurting:** We are
  called to be the hands and feet of Jesus, bringing
  healing and hope to those in need. Just as an ambulance responds to emergencies, we as the church must
  reach out to the broken and weary.

- **The power of striking the ground:** Striking the
  ground, as Elisha instructed Joash to do in 2 Kings 13,
  symbolizes faith in action. Every prayer and act of

obedience is like a strike to the ground. Even when
results aren't immediate, faith keeps us moving
forward.

- **God's provision through faith:** God responds to
  faith and obedience. The testimony of how God provided for the studio serves as a powerful reminder
  that He is faithful to fulfill His promises, even when
  the journey feels uncertain.

Personal Reflection

1. Take a moment to think about a time when you felt
   exhausted, discouraged, or ready to give up. Maybe
   it was a personal goal, a challenge in your family or
   relationships, or an area where you felt like God had
   promised something but weren't seeing results. What
   did you learn from that experience? Did you push
   through, or did you give up?

2. How can you apply the principle of unshakable faith to
   your current situation?

Group Discussion

1. I use the ambulance analogy to describe the church's
   mission. How does thinking of the church as a mobile
   hospital shape your view of our mission as believers?

2. The story of King Joash and the prophet Elisha
   in 2 Kings 13 teaches the importance of perseverance. Why do you think Elisha was upset when Joash
   stopped striking the ground after three times? How
   does this relate to your faith journey today?

3. How can we maintain unshakable faith when things aren't going as expected? Discuss specific challenges that you or others have faced where faith played a key role in helping you persevere.

4. Reflect on the story of the prophetic word I received about the studio and God's timely provision. How might trusting that God's timing is perfect strengthen the persistence needed to maintain unshakable faith?

APPLICATION

- **Think about your faith.** Meditate on the importance of being an active Christian.

- **Be an ambulance.** Remind yourself that there are multiple divine appointments each day. Think on how you can be the hands and feet of Jesus wherever you go.

- **Monitor your growth.** Celebrate small victories, and think of ways you can grow in unshakable faith.

ACTION PLAN FOR THE WEEK

- **Identify areas where your faith is weak.** Reflect on areas where your faith may have wavered. What are you tempted to give up on? Write down specific promises you feel God has spoken to you.

- **Persist in prayer.** Set aside time each day to pray for these weak areas. Commit to praying in faith, persevering even if you don't see immediate results.

- **Encourage someone.** As you build your faith, look for someone who may be struggling. Offer words of encouragement and pray for them. Remember, we are the hands and feet of Jesus, meant to lift up others in their faith.

- **Track your progress.** At the end of the week, write down any breakthroughs, shifts in your perspective, or moments of renewed strength you've gained as a result of walking in unshakable faith.

MEMORY VERSE

Let us not become weary in doing good, for at the proper time we will reap a harvest if we do not give up.

—GALATIANS 6:9

LIVING WITH ETERNITY IN MIND

I N A WORLD that moves at a rapid pace, we often focus on the immediate—what's happening right now, what we want right now, and how quickly we can get it. But everything changes when we look at life through the lens of eternity. We begin to see our possessions, our goals, and even our struggles in a new light. Living with eternity in mind shifts our priorities and redefines what truly matters.

KEY THEMES

- **The brevity of life:** The Bible reminds us that our time on earth is short, like a vapor that vanishes away (Jas. 4:14). This highlights the importance of keeping eternity in mind as we make decisions and live our lives.

- **What we take with us:** When we leave this earth, we can't take our possessions, wealth, or status with us. All that endures is our relationship with God and the treasures we store in heaven (Matt. 6:19–20).

- **Heavenly vs. earthly treasures:** Jesus teaches us to store treasures in heaven, where they are secure from decay and theft (Matt. 6:19–20). Earthly treasures are temporary, but heavenly treasures last forever.

- **The reality of eternity:** Living with eternity in mind means recognizing that our choices today have eternal consequences. The only way to eternal life is through Jesus Christ (John 14:6).

- **Living for what's eternal:** First John 2:17 reminds us, "The world is passing away, and also its lusts; but the one who does the will of God lives forever" (NASB). Pursuing temporary pleasures cannot fill the eternal void in our hearts. Only Jesus can satisfy it.

PERSONAL REFLECTION

1. Take a moment to think about your life. What do you prioritize on a daily basis? Is it your job, your possessions, your status, or something else?

2. Ask yourself, Are there things in my life that I'm holding on to tightly that I won't be able to take with me into eternity?

3. How does focusing on eternity change the way you view your day-to-day choices? Take a few minutes to reflect or to journal your thoughts.

GROUP DISCUSSION

1. Discuss the contrast between what's temporary—such as possessions, fame, and success—and what's eternal, such as faith and love. Which of these do we tend to prioritize in our lives and why?

2. In chapter 11, I use the analogy of an airport to describe our journey toward eternity. What do you think about this comparison? What does the TSA checkpoint represent in terms of our spiritual lives?

3. Are there any idols in your life that you need to let go of? How can we refocus our hearts on what is eternal?

4. What does living with an eternal perspective look like in everyday life? Share practical ways to begin storing up treasures in heaven rather than focusing on earthly treasures.

Application

- **Shift your focus.** Start recognizing the things that have eternal value. Begin to prioritize what matters most in the light of eternity.

- **Examine your idols.** Identify things in your life that you may be holding too tightly. Are you placing possessions or personal achievements above God's will for your life? Challenge yourself to surrender everything to God and shift your focus to Him.

- **Store treasures in heaven.** Instead of focusing on accumulating wealth or material possessions, think about ways you can invest in things that last forever. What can you do that has eternal significance, such as serving others, sharing the gospel, or making a difference in someone's life?

- **Live with purpose.** Remember that everything you do can have an eternal impact. Whether at work, at school, or in your relationships, live with a sense of purpose that aligns with God's will and focus on the eternal rather than the temporary.

ACTION PLAN FOR THE WEEK

- **Focus on eternal priorities.** Each day this week, ask God to help you focus on the things that have eternal significance.

- **Evaluate your attachments.** Take a few minutes to assess anyone or anything that may have become idols in your life. Write down at least one thing you feel called to release or reassess in order to prioritize God.

- **Share the gospel.** This week, share the hope you have in Christ with at least one person and tell them how living with eternity in mind shapes your perspective. Look for opportunities to be a light to others by sharing the message of eternal life through Jesus.

- **Plan for eternity.** Reflect on how your current actions, finances, and relationships can be used to build up treasures in heaven. Make a plan to adjust any areas where you're focusing too much on the temporary and not enough on the eternal.

MEMORY VERSE

For what will it profit a man if he gains the whole world and loses his own soul?

—MATTHEW 16:26, MEV

Appendix A

THE ANOINTING IS THE DIFFERENCE MAKER

G OD IS CALLING us to live by faith, but He doesn't expect us to do it on our own. He gives us the power to do so.

Jesus said in Acts 1:8, "But you shall receive power when the Holy Spirit has come upon you; and you shall be witnesses to Me in Jerusalem, and in all Judea and Samaria, and to the end of the earth" (NKJV). As Christians, we all will face situations and assignments that seem beyond our natural abilities. Whether it's sharing the gospel, ministering behind the pulpit, giving altar calls, or living a life that honors God, it will become clear that our own strength and gifts are not enough.

But here's the good news: The anointing of the Holy Spirit is the difference maker!

The anointing is simply *the yoke-destroying, burden-removing power of God* (Isa. 10:27). It is what empowers us to do what we cannot do on our own and to minister for Jesus beyond our natural abilities.

I want to share with you four ways the anointing of the Holy Spirit empowers us to be effective witnesses for the kingdom of God. The anointing is truly the power of God that makes all the difference.

1. The Anointing Empowers Us to Do the Impossible

In Acts 1:8 Jesus promised His disciples that they would receive power when the Holy Spirit came upon them. This was a guarantee that they would be equipped to do things beyond their own capacity. The Holy Spirit would make the difference, empowering them to be the hands and feet of Jesus and enabling them to accomplish His mission in ways they could not do on their own.

I've experienced this firsthand. I remember a time when I was catching a flight home after ministering at a conference in another state. I was running late, and when I finally made it to my gate, I felt a sense of relief as I boarded the plane. My seat was near the front, and I was eager to take a nap and wake up when we landed in Chicago.

A few minutes after settling in, a woman approached and asked if she could sit in the window seat. It was just the two of us in the row. As the plane took off, she started a conversation, telling me she was from Pakistan, studying for her PhD, and had a connecting flight in Chicago. We quickly found ourselves engaged in a deep discussion about our faiths—she shared her beliefs as a Muslim, and I shared mine as a Christian.

At one point I felt led to demonstrate the power behind what I was saying, as Scripture says, "The kingdom of God is not a matter of talk but of power" (1 Cor. 4:20). Paul also writes, "My message and my preaching were not with wise and persuasive words, but with a demonstration of the Spirit's power" (1 Cor. 2:4). I asked the woman if she had any pain in her body, and she mentioned that she had pain in her feet.

I offered to pray for her, but when I extended my hand, she looked at it and explained, "I'm sorry, but I cannot touch you unless you're a close family relative." I told her, "No problem at all," but in that moment I suddenly felt the anointing of the Holy Spirit stronger than before. She felt it too. Without a word, she removed the scarf from around her neck and draped it over my hand, saying, "You can pray now."

I was amazed and thanked her for her openness. I wanted to show her how the power of the Holy Spirit confirms the message of the gospel. She agreed, so I began. I said, "If your god is real, let him respond and heal your feet." Nothing happened. Then when I prayed in Jesus' name, immediately her eyes widened, and she said, "Why do my feet feel so hot? The pain is gone!"

We rejoiced together, and she was amazed by the power and authority in the name of Jesus. Right there on the plane the Holy Spirit began to fill her with joy. I even received words of knowledge about her youngest child, who could sing, and a friend named Ann she had been with earlier that day. All of this happened because of the anointing that made the difference!

The anointing of the Holy Spirit empowers us to go beyond mere words and into real, life-changing encounters. It opens doors that human effort cannot. It's the anointing that heals, transforms, and brings revelation. That's what made the difference on that plane. It wasn't just my words; it was His power working through me. And it was evident to both of us. The anointing is what makes the difference, every time!

Before the Holy Spirit came upon the disciples, they were fearful, confused, and unsure of how to continue Jesus' mission. Peter, who denied Jesus three times, would soon become a bold preacher.

Less than two months after denying the Lord, Peter was preaching openly and boldly to crowds of thousands. Consider this: On the day of Pentecost, about three thousand people got saved after hearing Peter preach (Acts 2:41). That's a thousand people for each time he denied the Lord. Amazing!

What made the difference? It was the anointing!

The Holy Spirit transformed ordinary men into extraordinary witnesses for Christ. And He wants to do the same with you!

The ministry of Jesus was centered around three key purposes: to seek and save the lost, to establish the kingdom of heaven on earth, and to destroy the works of the devil. As followers of Christ we are called to be "continuators" of His ministry, and to do so effectively we need the anointing and to be empowered by the Holy Spirit.

When we feel inadequate or timid, it's the anointing that makes the impossible possible. What you cannot do in your own strength you can do through the power of the Holy Spirit! As Zechariah 4:6 says, "'Not by might nor by power, but by My Spirit,' says the LORD of hosts" (NKJV).

2. THE ANOINTING GIVES US BOLDNESS

In Acts 4:31 the apostles prayed, and "when they had prayed, the place where they were assembled together was shaken; and they were all filled with the Holy Spirit, and they spoke the word of God with boldness" (NKJV).

Before the Holy Spirit came upon them, they were ordinary men filled with fears and uncertainties. But once the Holy Spirit empowered them, they preached with a boldness that was not their own.

If you've ever felt hesitant to share the gospel, afraid of rejection, or unsure of what to say, the anointing changes that. When the Holy Spirit comes upon you, He gives you boldness to do what you could never do in your own strength.

When you are filled with the Holy Spirit, you no longer rely on your own wisdom or ways. You speak with the authority and boldness of the Holy Spirit, who causes your words to carry weight. As we read in 2 Timothy 1:7, "For God has not given us a spirit of fear, but of power and of love and of a sound mind" (NKJV).

3. THE ANOINTING BRINGS SUPERNATURAL RESULTS

When the Holy Spirit is present, the results are supernatural. This was evident on the plane with that Muslim woman, and we see it clearly in Acts 10:38, which says, "God anointed Jesus of Nazareth with the Holy Spirit and with power, who went about doing good and healing all who were oppressed by the devil, for God was with Him" (NKJV).

Jesus didn't do His ministry in His own strength. He was anointed by the Holy Spirit, and it was this anointing that empowered Him to heal the sick, cast out demons, and perform miracles.

The same Holy Spirit that anointed Jesus is the Spirit who lives in you and me (Rom. 8:11)! When we minister under the anointing, we see God's power in ways we could never manufacture on our own. It is the anointing that makes the impossible possible.

Jesus declared in Luke 4:18, "The Spirit of the LORD is upon Me, because He has anointed Me to preach the gospel to the poor; He has sent Me to heal the brokenhearted, to proclaim liberty to the captives and recovery of sight to the blind, to set at liberty those who are oppressed" (NKJV).

4. THE ANOINTING ENABLES US TO LIVE HOLY LIVES

The anointing isn't just for ministry—it also helps you live a transformed life. It is the anointing of the Holy Spirit that empowers us to say no to our flesh and live lives pleasing to God.

Without the Holy Spirit, we will struggle to live a holy life. But with the anointing, we receive power to overcome sin, resist temptation, and walk in victory.

The anointing is your superpower. It's the difference maker in everything you do for Jesus!

Many people think this gift of the Holy Spirit is only for a select few or certain elite Christians. Scripture says this is a free gift available to all. Don't overthink it. Just ask Jesus to fill you and empower you with the Holy Spirit, and He will do it. He wants you to be filled even more than you want to be filled. It will take your prayer life to another level, and you will see the supernatural in your life. We need that power and anointing to be effective witnesses for Christ. Ask Him today to fill you!

THE GATE OF ETERNITY

O NE DAY AS I walked through an airport, listening to worship music, I suddenly felt God's presence so strongly. I looked around at all the people rushing to their gates, waiting to board flights to different destinations. In that moment God started showing me something about our journey toward eternity. Just like the people in the airport waiting at their gates, we are all headed toward a destination—eternity. But here's the thing: You can't board your flight without following the necessary procedures. You have to pass through the TSA checkpoint, follow the security protocols, and listen to the instructions of the airline. You can't skip those steps if you want to get on your plane. If you ignore the process, you won't make it through the gate.

God showed me that entering the kingdom of heaven is much the same. There's a process, a specific way to approach the gate of eternity. Jesus said in John 14:6, "I am the way and the truth and the life. No one comes to the Father except through me." Just as you can't reach your destination without going through the TSA checkpoint, you cannot bypass Jesus if you want to enter heaven. There's no other way.

Many people live good lives, help others, and strive to be kind, but good works alone won't get them into heaven. The only way to reach our eternal destination is through Jesus Christ. He is the gate, the only way to eternal life. If you haven't given your life to Him, I urge you to do so today. This is the most important decision you will ever make, and it has eternal consequences.

The Bible makes it clear that there is a specific way to approach the gate of eternity. In the same way you need to follow the airport's procedures to board your flight, you must follow the instructions given in God's Word to reach heaven. Imagine if someone tried to bypass TSA and just walked to their gate hoping to board a plane. They would be stopped because they haven't fulfilled the necessary requirements. You would never ignore airport security. Don't ignore the way to eternal life.

As you're finishing this book, I encourage you to take inventory. If you have never given your life to Jesus Christ, don't wait. It is so important and the greatest joy you could ever experience. Eternity hangs on the choice you make.

Romans 10:9 tells us, "If you declare with your mouth, 'Jesus is Lord,' and believe in your heart that God raised him from the dead, you will be saved." Jesus paid a high price for each of us. Sin separates us from God, but Jesus came to bridge that gap through His sacrifice on the cross.

While many religions involve man reaching for God, Christianity is unique in that it involves God reaching out to man. People have believed in many false gods throughout history, but only One has been proved by history: Jesus Christ. Only He conquered death, and only He rose again. Jesus bore the punishment we deserved, died in our place, and made a way for us to live in His victory. He took on our brokenness so we could take on His righteousness.

When God looks at the cross, He sees you and me. Every one of our wrongs, every failure, every weakness—Jesus took them all upon Himself. But here's the wonder of grace: When God looks at you, He sees Jesus.

As 2 Corinthians 5:21 says, "God made him who had no sin to be sin for us, so that in him we might become the righteousness of God." Through this divine exchange we can receive full forgiveness and be made new. We no longer need to carry the weight of our past. When we confess our sins, He is faithful and just to forgive us

(1 John 1:9). We are not defined by our mistakes anymore—we are defined by Christ.

This gift is freely offered to you. You don't have to earn it or prove yourself worthy. It's given out of pure love and grace. Will you give your life to Jesus today?

For those who have already made the decision to surrender your life to Christ, I encourage you to commit to living fully for Him. Follow Him, obey Him, and serve Him with all your heart today and always.

When you commit to Jesus, you are not merely standing at the gate—you are stepping onto the path that leads to your eternal home.

Salvation/Rededication Prayer

Heavenly Father, I take this moment to confess with my mouth and believe in my heart that Jesus Christ died on the cross for my sins and that You raised Him from the dead with all power. I repent of my sins and receive Your righteousness and forgiveness. From this day forward, I commit myself to follow You and obey You all the days of my life. Help me to live a life pleasing to You and to bear fruit for Your glory. In Jesus' name, amen.

If you've given your life to Christ or rededicated your life to Him, I encourage you to find a Bible-believing church where you can grow in your faith. Read your Bible daily, seek the Lord, and surround yourself with a community of believers. Let the Holy Spirit reveal more of Jesus to you and transform you into His image. This is vital to living a life that honors God. As you surrender your life to Him, He will guide you every step of the way.

PRAYING FOR YOUR LOST LOVED ONES

YEARS AGO, I was introduced to a powerful prayer that I want to share with you. It's a prayer you can use to intercede for those who have not yet given their lives to Jesus. I believe it will help you stand in faith for the salvation of these precious souls.

When praying for lost family members or friends, it's important to approach God with confidence, remembering this one key truth: God loves them even more than you do. His desire is that all people be saved and come to the knowledge of the truth (1 Tim. 2:4)—and that includes your loved ones.

I once read something that deeply impacted my understanding of prayer for the lost. It said one of the most significant factors in a person's salvation is the influence of believers like you and me. Jesus told us to pray to the Lord of the harvest, asking Him to send laborers into His fields (Luke 10:2). This means you can pray for God to send the right person to your loved one—someone who can share the gospel in a way they will understand and respond to.

As you pray for your loved ones, remember that your prayers make a difference. James 5:16 assures us that "the prayer of a righteous person is powerful and effective." When you pray, you open the door for God's power to work in their hearts.

Finally, don't be discouraged by what you see in the natural. Walk by faith, not by sight. Trust God, and thank Him in advance for encountering your loved ones with His power and love.

Here is a prayer you can use as a guide to pray for your loved one.

SAMPLE PRAYER FOR YOUR UNSAVED LOVED ONE

Father, Your Word says that You desire for all people to be saved and come to the knowledge of the truth. So today, I lift up _____ before You. In the name of Jesus, I break the power of the enemy over _____'s life and all of [his/her] assignments.

I ask You, Lord, to send the right people into _____'s life to share the gospel in a way that [he/she] will listen to and understand.

As Your truth is shared, I believe _____ will open [his/her] heart to the message of the gospel, come out of the devil's snare, and make Jesus Lord of [his/her] life.

Father, I ask You to fill _____ with the knowledge of Your will, in all wisdom and spiritual understanding. As I pray for _____ today, I believe the power of the Holy Spirit is working in [his/her] life, and I thank You for it.

From this moment on, I choose to praise You for _____'s salvation. I am confident that You are actively watching over Your Word to perform it.

Therefore, I declare in faith: God has begun a good work in _____'s life, and He will bring it to completion until the day of Jesus Christ. In Jesus' name, amen.

PRAYING FOR PERSECUTED CHRISTIANS AROUND THE WORLD

FELT IT WAS necessary to shed light on all the Christians around the world who are facing severe persecution for their faith, with millions suffering in silence. According to Open Doors USA, more than 380 million Christians live in places where they experience high levels of persecution and discrimination.[1] Every day, believers in countries such as North Korea, Afghanistan, Somalia, and Nigeria risk their lives for the simple act of worshipping Jesus.

Many are forced to flee their homes, imprisoned, tortured, or even killed because of their faith. I read that in some regions, entire communities are displaced and families are torn apart. Despite all these things, Christians continue to boldly proclaim the gospel, showing so much courage in the face of intense suffering.

According to 2025 statistics from Open Doors:

- 380 million Christians experience high levels of persecution worldwide.

- North Korea remains the most dangerous place for Christians, where believers risk imprisonment, torture, and death.

- More than 4,000 Christians were killed last year because of their faith in God.

- Last year, more than 200,000 Christians were forced to flee their homes and go into hiding or exile.[2]

As believers in Christ we are called to stand with our brothers and sisters around the world, lifting them up in prayer, offering support, and advocating for their freedom. The Bible tells us to remember those who are persecuted as if we were suffering alongside them (Heb. 13:3). May we be a voice for the voiceless and pray for God's protection, strength, and peace over their lives.

Prayer for Persecuted Christians

Heavenly Father, we come before You today, burdened for our brothers and sisters around the world who are suffering for their faith. We lift them up to You, asking for Your hedge of protection, Your strength, and the blood of Jesus. Lord, where they face violence and oppression, cover them with Your peace that passes understanding. Where they endure isolation, surround them with Your love, reminding them they are never alone.

We pray for those who are imprisoned for their faith, that You would open doors for their release. For those in danger of death or imprisonment, give them the courage to stand firm in the truth of the gospel. For those who have lost loved ones, comfort them with Your presence and restore their hope.

Lord, we ask that You strengthen the global church so that we may stand together in prayer and action. Stir in us a spirit of compassion and boldness to speak up for those who cannot. May we never forget those who suffer in silence.

We thank You for the faithfulness of these believers, and we pray for Your provision, protection, and peace to rest upon them today and always. In Jesus' name, amen.

I recommend learning more about persecuted Christians and how to support them. I have been following @marchforthemartyrs online for years and would encourage believers to get involved with them.

NOTES

Chapter 3

1. Bible Hub, s.v. *"Gethsémani,"* accessed February 10, 2025, https://biblehub.com/greek/1068.htm.

Chapter 5

1. Blue Letter Bible, s.v. *"hănanyâ,"* accessed February 10, 2025, https://www.blueletterbible.org/lexicon/h2608/kjv/wlc/0-1/; Bible Hub, s.v. "Shadrak," accessed February 10, 2025, https://biblehub.com/hebrew/7714.htm.
2. Blue Letter Bible, s.v. *"mîšā'ēl,"* accessed February 10, 2025, https://www.blueletterbible.org/lexicon/h4332/kjv/wlc/0-1/; Wikipedia, s.v. "Shadrach, Meshach, and Abednego," last edited February 2, 2025, https://en.wikipedia.org/wiki/Shadrach,_Meshach,_and_Abednego.
3. Blue Letter Bible, s.v. *"'ăzaryâ,"* accessed February 10, 2025, https://www.blueletterbible.org/lexicon/h5838/kjv/wlc/0-1/; Blue Letter Bible, s.v. *"abed-negô,"* accessed February 10, 2025, https://www.blueletterbible.org/lexicon/h5664/kjv/wlc/0-1/.

Chapter 6

1. A. W. Tozer, *I Talk Back to the Devil: The Fighting Fervor of the Victorious Christian* (Moody Publishers, 2008).

2. "The State of Church Attendance: Trends and Statistics [2024]," ChurchTrac, accessed February 10, 2025, https://www.churchtrac.com/articles/the-state-of-church-attendance-trends-and-statistics-2023?utm_source=chatgpt.com; "Silent and Solo: How Americans Pray," Barna Group, August 15, 2017, https://www.barna.com/research/silent-solo-americans-pray/?utm_source=chatgpt.com.

3. Aleksandra Sandstrom and Commodo Duis, "Church Involvement Varies Widely Among US Christians," Pew Research Center, November 16, 2015, https://www.pewresearch.org/short-reads/2015/11/16/church-involvement-varies-widely-among-u-s-christians/; "New Research on the State of Discipleship," Barna Group, December 1, 2015, https://www.barna.com/research/new-research-on-the-state-of-discipleship/.

4. American Bible Society, "American Bible Society's New Study Shows Urgent Ministry Opportunity with 'Bible Explorers,'" PR Newswire, April 6, 2023, https://www.prnewswire.com/news-releases/american-bible-societys-new-study-shows-urgent-ministry-opportunity-with-bible-explorers-301791741.html.

Chapter 11

1. "I Think Everybody Should Get Rich and Famous So They Can See That That's Not the Answer," Quote Investigator, November 9, 2022, https://quoteinvestigator.com/2022/11/09/rich-famous/.

Appendix D

1. "Open Doors World Watch List 2025," Open Doors USA, accessed February 10, 2025, https://www.opendoorsus.

org/en-US/getinvolved/resources/wwl-booklets/2025-wwl-booklet-digital.

2. "Open Doors World Watch List 2025," Open Doors USA.

ABOUT THE AUTHOR

MATT CRUZ WAS born and raised in a multicultural church on the South Side of Chicago, where his parents serve as senior assistant pastors. Matt grew up in ministry but didn't fully experience the transformative power of God early in his life. After attempting paths in law enforcement and the military, an encounter with the Holy Spirit in his basement at nineteen years old changed the course of his life.

Matt's passion for evangelism led him to the streets of Chicago, where he saw countless people come to Christ and experience the power of God. His social media videos showing him witnessing and encouraging others have reached over 200 million viewers.

Nearly a decade after he told his parents he would never preach, Matt has become a dynamic voice in churches and conferences across the United States and is the host of the annual RiseUpRevival conference in Chicago every fall. He has been featured on *Sid Roth's It's Supernatural!* and has appeared on numerous programs and podcasts, sharing the Word of God and his powerful testimony alongside seasoned ministers in the body of Christ.

Matt is widely recognized for his dynamic preaching and genuine heart, inspiring people to live fully for God and experience the transformative power of the Holy Spirit.

THANK YOU FOR READING

I PRAY THIS BOOK has been a blessing to you and that it has stirred your heart to anchor your faith in Jesus and live for Him wholeheartedly. I encourage you to put the Scriptures into practice and stay connected to the Vine, for this is the key to bearing lasting fruit and living fully in Him. Cultivate the fire in your heart and offer yourself daily on the altar.

While reading books and attending conferences to receive inspiration from guest speakers can be valuable, they should never replace our personal responsibility to nurture our faith each day. Don't settle for temporary experiences or rely on others to constantly fuel your faith. True spiritual maturity calls us to move from being spectators to becoming flame keepers.

One thing I have learned is that relying solely on books, conferences, and guest speakers for spiritual fire is like eating only when we're invited to a banquet. But what happens when the banquet is over? We starve. Without intentionally nurturing our faith, we will find ourselves spiritually famished. Stay connected to the Vine, and keep the fire burning in your own heart.

PARTNER WITH US

Matt Cruz Ministries and our studio headquarters are fully supported by the generosity of partners and donors. Would you consider making a one-time gift or becoming a monthly partner? Your support helps us continue traveling full-time and sustaining all that God is doing at the headquarters through worship, discipleship nights, and the teaching of His Word.

www.mattcruzministries.com/partner

STAY CONNECTED

Facebook.com/matt.cruz.146

Instagram: @MattCruz96

YouTube: @MattCruz

mattcruzministries.com